PLAY ON SHAKESPEARE

Antony and Cleopatra

PLAY ON SHAKESPEARE

All's Well That Ends Well	Virginia Grise
Antony and Cleopatra	Christopher Chen
As You Like It	David Ivers
The Comedy of Errors	Christina Anderson
Coriolanus	Sean San José
Cymbeline	Andrea Thome
Edward III	Octavio Solis
Hamlet	Lisa Peterson
Henry IV	Yvette Nolan
Henry V	Lloyd Suh
Henry VI	Douglas P. Langworthy
Henry VIII	Caridad Svich
Julius Caesar	Shishir Kurup
King John	Brighde Mullins
King Lear	Marcus Gardley
Love's Labour's Lost	Josh Wilder
Macbeth	Migdalia Cruz
Measure for Measure	Aditi Brennan Kapil
The Merchant of Venice	Elise Thoron
The Merry Wives of Windsor	Dipika Guha
A Midsummer Night's Dream	Jeffrey Whitty
Much Ado About Nothing	Ranjit Bolt
Othello	Mfoniso Udofia
Pericles	Ellen McLaughlin
Richard II	Naomi Iizuka
Richard III	Migdalia Cruz
Romeo and Juliet	Hansol Jung
The Taming of the Shrew	Amy Freed
The Tempest	Kenneth Cavander
Timon of Athens	Kenneth Cavander
Titus Andronicus	Amy Freed
Troilus and Cressida	Lillian Groag
Twelfth Night	Alison Carey
The Two Gentlemen of Verona	Amelia Roper
The Two Noble Kinsmen	Tim Slover
The Winter's Tale	Tracy Young

Antony and Cleopatra

by
William Shakespeare

Modern verse translation by
Christopher Chen

Dramaturgy by
Desdemona Chiang

Arizona State University
Tempe, Arizona
2023

———

Publication of Play On Shakespeare is assisted by
generous support from the Hitz Foundation.
For more information, please visit www.playonshakespeare.org

———

Published by ACMRS Press
Arizona Center for Medieval and Renaissance Studies,
Arizona State University, Tempe, Arizona
www.acmrspress.com

Library of Congress Cataloging-in-Publication Data

Names: Chen, Christopher (Christopher Albert), author. | Chiang,
   Desdemona, contributor. | Shakespeare, William, 1564–1616. Antony and
   Cleopatra.
Title: Antony and Cleopatra / by William Shakespeare ; modern verse
   translation by Christopher Chen ; dramaturgy by Desdemona Chiang.
Description: Tempe, Arizona : ACMRS Press, 2023. | Series: Play on
   Shakespeare | Summary: "This lively contemporary translation of
   Shakespeare's sexiest play brings the political intrigue and historical
   storytelling to modern audiences while preserving the poetic foundation of
   the play's language"-- Provided by publisher.
Identifiers: LCCN 2023030614 (print) | LCCN 2023030615 (ebook) | ISBN
   9780866987899 (paperback) | ISBN 9780866987905 (ebook)
Subjects: LCSH: Antonius, Marcus, 83 B.C.?-30 B.C.--Drama. | Cleopatra,
   Queen of Egypt, -30 B.C.--Drama. | Romans--Egypt--Drama. | Rome--
   History--Civil War, 43-31 B.C.--Drama. | Egypt--History--332-30 B.C.--
   Drama. | LCGFT: Tragedies (Drama) | Historical drama.
Classification: LCC PR2878.A5 C44 2023 (print) | LCC PR2878.A5 (ebook) |
   DDC 822.3/3--dc23/eng/20230705
LC record available at https://lccn.loc.gov/2023030614
LC ebook record available at https://lccn.loc.gov/2023030615
Printed in the United States of America

We wish to acknowledge our gratitude
for the extraordinary generosity of the
Hitz Foundation

∼

Special thanks to the Play on Shakespeare staff
Lue Douthit, President and Co-Founder
Taylor Bailey, Producing Director
Cheryl Rizzo, Business Director
Artie Calvert, Finance Director

∼

Originally commissioned by the
Oregon Shakespeare Festival
Bill Rauch, Artistic Director
Cynthia Rider, Executive Director

PLAY ON SHAKESPEARE

In 2015, the Oregon Shakespeare Festival announced a new commissioning program. It was called "Play on!: 36 playwrights translate Shakespeare." It elicited a flurry of reactions. For some people this went too far: "You can't touch the language!" For others, it didn't go far enough: "Why not new adaptations?" I figured we would be on the right path if we hit the sweet spot in the middle.

Some of the reaction was due not only to the scale of the project, but its suddenness: 36 playwrights, along with 38 dramaturgs, had been commissioned and assigned to translate 39 plays, and they were already hard at work on the assignment. It also came fully funded by the Hitz Foundation with the shocking sticker price of $3.7 million.

I think most of the negative reaction, however, had to do with the use of the word "translate." It's been difficult to define precisely. It turns out that there is no word for the kind of subtle and rigorous examination of language that we are asking for. We don't mean "word for word," which is what most people think of when they hear the word translate. We don't mean "paraphrase," either.

The project didn't begin with 39 commissions. Linguist John McWhorter's musings about translating Shakespeare is what sparked this project. First published in his 1998 book *Word on the Street* and reprinted in 2010 in *American Theatre* magazine, he notes that the "irony today is that the Russians, the French, and other people in foreign countries possess Shakespeare to a much greater extent than we do, for the simple reason that they get to enjoy Shakespeare in the language they speak."

This intrigued Dave Hitz, a long-time patron of the Oregon Shakespeare Festival, and he offered to support a project that looked at Shakespeare's plays through the lens of the English we speak today. How much has the English language changed since Shakespeare? Is it possible that there are conventions in the early modern English of Shakespeare that don't translate to us today, especially in the moment of hearing it spoken out loud as one does in the theater?

How might we "carry forward" the successful communication between actor and audience that took place 400 years ago? "Carry forward," by the way, is what we mean by "translate." It is the fourth definition of *translate* in the Oxford English Dictionary.

As director of literary development and dramaturgy at the Oregon Shakespeare Festival, I was given the daunting task of figuring out how to administer the project. I began with Kenneth Cavander, who translates ancient Greek tragedies into English. I figured that someone who does that kind of work would lend an air of seriousness to the project. I asked him how might he go about translating from the source language of early modern English into the target language of contemporary modern English?

He looked at different kinds of speech: rhetorical and poetical, soliloquies and crowd scenes, and the puns in comedies. What emerged from his tinkering became a template for the translation commission. These weren't rules exactly, but instructions that every writer was given.

First, do no harm. There is plenty of the language that doesn't need translating. And there is some that does. Every playwright had different criteria for assessing what to change.

Second, go line-by-line. No editing, no cutting, no "fixing." I want the whole play translated. We often cut the gnarly bits in

Shakespeare for performance. What might we make of those bits if we understood them in the moment of hearing them? Might we be less compelled to cut?

Third, all other variables stay the same: the time period, the story, the characters, their motivations, and their thoughts. We designed the experiment to examine the language.

Fourth, and most important, the language must follow the same kind of rigor and pressure as the original, which means honoring the meter, rhyme, rhetoric, image, metaphor, character, action, and theme. Shakespeare's astonishingly compressed language must be respected. Trickiest of all: making sure to work within the structure of the iambic pentameter.

We also didn't know which of Shakespeare's plays might benefit from this kind of investigation: the early comedies, the late tragedies, the highly poetic plays. So we asked three translators who translate plays from other languages into English to examine a Shakespeare play from each genre outlined in the *First Folio*: Kenneth took on *Timon of Athens,* a tragedy; Douglas Langworthy worked on the *Henry the Sixth* history plays, and Ranjit Bolt tried his hand at the comedy *Much Ado about Nothing.*

Kenneth's *Timon* received a production at the Alabama Shakespeare in 2014 and it was on the plane ride home that I thought about expanding the project to include 39 plays. And I wanted to do them all at once. The idea was to capture a snapshot of contemporary modern English. I couldn't oversee that many commissions, and when Ken Hitz (Dave's brother and president of the Hitz Foundation) suggested that we add a dramaturg to each play, the plan suddenly unfolded in front of me. The next day, I made a simple, but extensive, proposal to Dave on how to commission and develop 39 translations in three years. He responded immediately with "Yes."

My initial thought was to only commission translators who translate plays. But I realized that "carry forward" has other meanings. There was a playwright in the middle of the conversation 400 years ago. What would it mean to carry *that* forward?

For one thing, it would mean that we wanted to examine the texts through the lens of performance. I am interested in learning how a dramatist makes sense of the play. Basically, we asked the writers to create performable companion pieces.

I wanted to tease out what we mean by contemporary modern English, and so we created a matrix of writers who embodied many different lived experiences: age, ethnicity, gender-identity, experience with translations, geography, English as a second language, knowledge of Shakespeare, etc.

What the playwrights had in common was a deep love of language and a curiosity about the assignment. Not everyone was on board with the idea and I was eager to see how the experiment would be for them. They also pledged to finish the commission within three years.

To celebrate the completion of the translations, we produced a festival in June 2019 in partnership with The Classic Stage Company in New York to hear all 39 of them. Four hundred years ago I think we went to *hear* a play; today we often go to *see* a play. In the staged reading format of the Festival, we heard these plays as if for the first time. The blend of Shakespeare with another writer was seamless and jarring at the same time. Countless actors and audience members told us that the plays were understandable in ways they had never been before.

Now it's time to share the work. We were thrilled when Ayanna Thompson and her colleagues at the Arizona Center for Medieval and Renaissance Studies offered to publish the translations for us.

I ask that you think of these as marking a moment in time.

The editions published in this series are based on the scripts that were used in the Play on! Festival in 2019. For the purpose of the readings, there were cuts allowed and these scripts represent those reading drafts.

The original commission tasked the playwrights and dramaturg to translate the whole play. The requirement of the commission was for two drafts which is enough to put the ball in play. The real fun with these texts is when there are actors, a director, a dramaturg, and the playwright wrestling with them together in a rehearsal room.

The success of a project of this scale depends on the collaboration and contributions of many people. The playwrights and dramaturgs took the assignment seriously and earnestly and were humble and gracious throughout the development of the translations. Sally Cade Holmes and Holmes Productions, our producer since the beginning, provided a steady and calm influence.

We have worked with more than 1,200 artists in the development of these works. We have partnered with more than three dozen theaters and schools. Numerous readings and more than a dozen productions of these translations have been heard and seen in the United States as well as Canada, England, and the Czech Republic.

There is a saying in the theater that 80% of the director's job is taken care of when the production is cast well. Such was my luck when I hired Taylor Bailey, who has overseen every reading and workshop, and was the producer of the Festival in New York. Katie Kennedy has gathered all the essays, and we have been supported by the rest of the Play on Shakespeare team: Kamilah Long, Summer Martin, and Amrita Ramanan.

All of this has come to be because Bill Rauch, then artistic director of the Oregon Shakespeare Festival, said yes when Dave

Hitz pitched the idea to him in 2011. Actually he said, "Hmm, interesting," which I translated to "yes." I am dearly indebted to that 'yes.'

My gratitude to Dave, Ken, and the Hitz Foundation can never be fully expressed. Their generosity, patience, and unwavering belief in what we are doing has given us the confidence to follow the advice of Samuel Beckett: "Ever tried. Ever failed. No matter. Try again. Fail again. Fail better."

Play on!

Dr. Lue Douthit
CEO/Creative Director at Play on Shakespeare
October 2020

WHAT WAS I THINKING?

Below is the transcript of a conversation between playwright Christopher Chen and dramaturg Desdemona Chiang, about their experience working on the Play On! translation of Antony and Cleopatra, *and a brief look into of one of the excerpts from the script.*

DES: So. Why *Antony and Cleopatra*? What drew you to choosing this piece for Play On?

CHRIS: I love working with scale. I was attracted to the idea of wrestling with a great sweeping romance, larger than life characters, political intrigue, and historical storytelling on this epic canvas. I also wanted to explore one of the greatest characters in history — a complicated and powerful queen caught between her love for Antony and trying to save herself and her kingdom.

DES: Did you have an agenda in mind when approaching the text? Other than the obvious Play On directive to "do no harm"?

CHRIS: My goal was to have crystal clear audience comprehension in real time while maintaining as much Shakespeare as possible. I wanted to see how many distinct words and phrases I could keep while massaging some of the "sinew" — the interconnecting words — between them. And coupled with that, in keeping iambic pentameter retention, the language wanted to be as easy in the mouths of actors as possible.

DES: I'd love to dive into the text and get a bit in your head about how you arrived at certain translation decisions. Let's take this passage from Act 5, Scene 1 — one of my favorite monologues from Cleopatra, where she's essentially describing Antony and his greatness. Here is the original text:

> His legs bestrid the ocean; his reared arm
> Crested the world; his voice was propertied
> As all the tunèd spheres, and that to friends;
> But when he meant to quail and shake the orb,
> He was as rattling thunder. For his bounty,
> There was no winter in't; an autumn it was
> That grew the more by reaping. His delights
> Were dolphin-like: they showed his back above
> The element they lived in. In his livery
> Walked crowns and crownets; realms and islands were
> As plates dropped from his pocket.

This speech is a perfect example of how I feel when I read Shakespeare — it's very emotionally evocative, but when I actually think about it, I find that I don't know what half of these images really are. Autumn? Dolphins? It ends up being a wash of feelings that are powerful, but vague. And I certainly don't get any crystal-clear, real-time comprehension. How did you even begin to tackle this?

CHRIS: More often than not, I tended to err on the side of leaving language intact. I knew there were phrases I felt strongly about keeping — for example, "rattling thunder," which is so passionately Shakespearean to me. So I would try to preserve those whenever I could. Also, I found that by changing *one* word, you could leave other words in place. I change "bestrid" to "straddled," then I feel "reared arm crested the world" makes sense in context.

DES: What about parts of the speech that are more challenging? How much do you intervene? Like this line:

For his bounty
There was no winter in't; an autumn it was
That grew the more by reaping.

CHRIS: Oh, yeah. That was a tricky one. Especially the last part — an autumn that "grew the more by reaping." I remember we had to dive deep into research to untangle that one. This is what I arrived at:

His kindness was a harvest with no winter,
A strange and endless autumn which produced
More bounty by its reaping.

I was trying to clarify the metaphor itself. The idea was that this particular Autumn, when you reap your harvest, it actually grows *more* — it's a *weird* thing. So I added the word "strange" in there to emphasize that this is an extraordinary event. So in this case, where the language is a bit more knotty, it did require more work.

DES: Right — even though Mr. Shakespeare never explicitly uses an adjective like "strange" to describe the autumn, the idea of it being unusual is a key part to understanding that phrase. "Endless" also helps us understand that it's a never-ending phenomenon — Antony's kindness is infinite.

CHRIS: And I wanted to keep the word "bounty" — that feeling of abundance was important — so I just moved it a few lines down.

DES: So, in the end, here is our side-by-side:

SHAKESPEARE:

His legs bestrid the ocean; his reared arm
Crested the world; his voice was propertied
As all the tunèd spheres, and that to friends;
But when he meant to quail and shake the orb,
He was as rattling thunder. For his bounty,
There was no winter in 't; an autumn it was
That grew the more by reaping. His delights
Were dolphin-like: they showed his back above
The element they lived in. In his livery
Walked crowns and crownets; realms and islands were
As plates dropped from his pocket.

CHEN:

His legs straddled the ocean; his reared arm
Crested the world; his voice was harmonied
As all the well-tuned spheres, but when he meant
To shake the earth he was as rattling thunder.
His kindness was a harvest with no winter:
A strange and endless autumn which produced
More bounty by its reaping. His delights
Were dolphin-like: they leapt and bared themselves
Above the sea of war he swam in. Kings
And princes served him; realms and islands were
As change dropped from his pocket.

CHRIS: In an earlier draft, I had at one point translated "his voice was propertied" [in the second line of the speech] to "his voice harmonious," but then ended up changing it to "his voice was harmonied" to match the original's rhythm. Which isn't a real word!

DES: You know, when the content makes sense to me, my brain

doesn't care if the word is real. "Harmonied" sounds like "harmonized," but scans way better. Shakespeare made up tons of words for the sake of poetic license.

CHRIS: Shakespeare cheats sometimes! In order to make the meter fit, he'll take out words here and there so that the language sounds good!

DES: I wonder sometimes if our admiration and appreciation for Shakespeare comes from the fact that the material isn't always entirely clear. Like the way I'm biased towards operas not sung in English. Do we make the play less appealing by making it more comprehensible?

CHRIS: Shakespeare's metaphors are so interesting and complex, that I think even when they're translated, they still feel mysterious and somewhat out of our reach. His visual descriptions are so rich and beyond the pedestrian realm. Audiences may still have to think about them, except now with the translation you have a fighting chance.

DES: I remember when we did our workshop presentation at Seattle Rep, Lue did this fabulous "side-by-side" exercise with the audience where she presented excerpts of the script, and people often couldn't tell the difference between your translation and the original Shakespeare.

CHRIS: And that was the highest compliment, because that was the thing you and I were both going for. I considered myself a craftsperson, just keeping the audience, the actors, and Shakespeare's words in mind. I was purposefully putting none of my own artistry in it.

DES: What does that feel like, as a dramatist, to be writing a piece and not generating material — to be more of a "craftsperson" in this case, as you say?

CHRIS: There was a bit of a self-imposed — or maybe socially imposed? — pressure that I felt, because it was *Shakespeare*. But the exercise itself was actually quite delightful. I've always loved Shakespeare, but here I felt like I really got to experience his genius anew — and even though my assignment was to make his work "clearer," his poetry is so well-wrought, that in order to honor the poetry I felt like I was also becoming a "poetic" playwright, which I never used to consider myself.

DES: I totally think you're a poetic playwright! Maybe not in the conventional highfalutin way we think of when we think of Shakespeare — I personally think he can be somewhat decorative — but you have an essentialism that I find to be quite poetic.

CHRIS: I think I used to be a very language-focused writer — I admired playwrights like Beckett and Sarah Kane, who are so precise in their language. But at a certain point in my career I shifted, and I started to care less about how exact the words looked on the page, and more about how they felt in the actors' mouths — that became more important.

DES: And that's what Shakespeare was in his time as well, he wrote for a company of actors.

CHRIS: Yes! And that's why this task was uniquely satisfying for me.

CHARACTERS IN THE PLAY

(in order of speaking)

PHILO, a member of Antony's party

CLEOPATRA, Queen of Egypt

ANTONY, Roman general and one of the three joint leaders, or "triumvirs," who rule the Roman Republic after the assassination of Julius Caesar

DEMETRIUS, a member of Antony's party

CHARMIAN, Cleopatra's maid of honor

ALEXAS, a member of Cleopatra's party

SOOTHSAYER

ENOBARBUS, a member of Antony's party

IRAS, Cleopatra's maid of honor

MESSENGER

3 MESSENGER

OCTAVIUS CAESAR, another triumvir

LEPIDUS, another triumvir

2 MESSENGER

MARDIAN, a eunuch

SEXTUS POMPEY, rebel against the triumvirate and son of the late Pompey

MENECRATES, a member of Pompey's party

MENAS, a member of Pompey's party

VARRIUS, a member of Pompey's party

MAECENAS, a member of Caesar's party

AGRIPPA, admiral of the Roman navy

OCTAVIA, Caesar's sister

EROS, a member of Antony's party

CANIDIUS, Antony's lieutenant-general

TAURUS, Caesar's lieutenant general

SCARUS, a member of Antony's party

DOLABELLA, a member of Caesar's party

AMBASSADOR, Antony's schoolmaster

THIDIAS, a member of Caesar's party

1 SOLDIER

2 SOLDIER

3 SOLDIER

SENTRY

1 WATCH

2 WATCH

1 GUARD

2 GUARD

3 GUARD

DERCETUS, a member of Antony's party

DIOMEDES, Cleopatra's treasurer

PROCULEIUS, a member of Caesar's party

CLOWN

GALLUS, a member of Caesar's party (non-speaking role)

Other **Eunuchs, Attendants, Ladies, Officers, Servants, Soldiers, Captains,** a **Guardsman,** and an **Egyptian**

ACT 1 ♦ SCENE 1

Enter Demetrius and Philo

PHILO

No, this infatuation of our General's
Now overruns all measures. His keen eyes,
Which once glowed like the God of War when scanning
His ranks of troops, now bend, now turn away
From this great face of war toward a face   5
Of darkened skin. His captain's heart, which once
Within the frenzy of grand melees burst
The buckles on his breastplate, now disowns
Its steel resolve to play the cooling fans
Of an Egyptian's lust.   10

Flourish

Enter Antony, Cleopatra, her ladies (Charmian and Iras),
the train, with Eunuchs fanning her

Look, here they come:
Now take good note, and you will see in him
The ruler of a third of the whole world
Transformed into a strumpet's fool: Behold.

CLEOPATRA

If it is love indeed, tell me how much.   15

ANTONY

There's poverty in love that can be measured.

CLEOPATRA

I'll set the boundaries on how far you love.

ANTONY

Then you must find new heaven, and new earth.

Enter an Attendant

1

ATTENDANT

News, my good lord, from Rome.

ANTONY

Grates me! Be brief.   20

CLEOPATRA

No, hear them, Antony:

Is Fulvia your wife not pleased? Or has

The scarce-bearded Caesar not sent a firm

Command to you: "Do this, or this; conquer

That kingdom, liberate that one; perform   25

For me or I'll damn you!"

ANTONY

What are you saying?

CLEOPATRA

It's some command. Most certainty you're called.

You must not stay, your marching orders come

From Caesar; therefore hear it, Antony.   30

What's Fulvia's mandate? Caesar's, I mean. Both?

Call in the messengers. As I am Egypt's queen,

You blush, dear Antony; with blood that bows

To young Caesar; unless your cheek pays shame

When shrill-tongued Fulvia scolds. The messengers!   35

ANTONY

Let Rome in Tiber melt, and the wide arch of

The ordered empire fall! Here is my space.

Kingdoms are clay! Our muddy earth feeds beasts

And men alike: the nobleness of life

Is to do this; when equals like us pair   40

And such a pair can do it. I command

The world to recognize our love, in which

We stand here peerless.

CLEOPATRA

What an excellent lie!

For did he not love Fulvia when they wed? 45

I'll seem the fool I'm not, and Antony

Will be the man he is.

ANTONY

And I am most myself with Cleopatra.

Now, for the love of Love and her soft hours,

Let's not confound the time with harsh conference: 50

There's not a minute of our lives should stretch

Without some pleasure now. What games tonight?

CLEOPATRA

Hear the messengers.

ANTONY

Damn you, quarrelsome queen!

Whose every act — to chide, to laugh, to weep — 55

Whose every passion fully strives in you

To make itself a fair and beauteous thing.

No messenger, just you. And all alone

Tonight we'll wander through the streets disguised

And mingle with the people. Come, my queen; 60

Last night you wished it: No more messengers.

Exit Mark Antony and Cleopatra with their train

DEMETRIUS

Is young Caesar so low in his esteem?

PHILO

Sir, sometimes, when he's not quite Antony,

Esteem and judgment don't quite reach the heights

That should still go with Antony. 65

DEMETRIUS

It's sad

That he lives down to gossip, sanctioning

This sketch of him they paint in Rome. I'll hope
Of better conduct in the morning. Rest well.

Exit

ACT 1 ♦ SCENE 2

Enter Enobarbus (and other Roman Officers), a Soothsayer,
Charmian, Iras, Mardian the Eunuch, and Alexas

CHARMIAN

Lord Alexas, sweet Alexas, most anything Alexas, almost
most absolute Alexas, where's the soothsayer you recom-
mended to the Queen? I was foretold a champion cuckold
for a husband who would wear his crown with pride.

ALEXAS

Soothsayer!   5

SOOTHSAYER

How may I serve?

CHARMIAN

Is this the man? Is it you, sir, who knows things?

SOOTHSAYER

In nature's infinite book of secrecy
A little I can read.

ALEXAS

Show him your hand.   10

ENOBARBUS

Bring in the food quickly; and enough wine
To toast Cleopatra's health.

Enter Servants with wine and other refreshments and exit

CHARMIAN *(gives her hand to the Soothsayer)*

Good sir, give me good fortune.

SOOTHSAYER

I give not, but foresee.

CHARMIAN

Please then, foresee me one. 15

SOOTHSAYER

You will be far fairer than you are now.

CHARMIAN

He means I'll be plump and well fed.

IRAS

No, you'll use too much makeup when you're old.

CHARMIAN

Oh, wrinkles!

ALEXAS

Don't disturb him. Be attentive. 20

CHARMIAN

Hush!

SOOTHSAYER

You will be more beloving than beloved.

CHARMIAN

I'd rather heat my loins with drinking.

ALEXAS

Stop! Hear him.

CHARMIAN

Come now, some excellent fortune! Let me be married to 25
three kings in a morning and widow them all. Let me have a
child at fifty. Tell me I'll marry Octavius Caesar and make me
equals with my mistress.

SOOTHSAYER

You will outlive the lady whom you serve.

CHARMIAN

Oh, excellent! I love long life better than figs. 30
Tell me, how many boys and girls will I have?

SOOTHSAYER

If each wish for a child of yours had womb,

You'd have a million children.

CHARMIAN

Out, fool!

ALEXAS

You think only your sheets can hear you.   35

CHARMIAN

No, come, tell Iras hers.

ALEXAS

We'll all know our fortunes.

ENOBARBUS

The fortunes of me and most others, will be *drunk to bed.*

IRAS *(holds out her hand)*

My palm predicts chastity, if nothing else.

CHARMIAN

If your oiled palm shows chastity, then my ears do deceive me.   40
Please, tell her a more trivial fortune.

SOOTHSAYER

Your fortunes are alike.

IRAS

But how, but how? Give me particulars!

SOOTHSAYER

I have said already.

IRAS

Am I not an inch of fortune better than she?   45

CHARMIAN

Well, if you were an inch more fortunate than I, where would
you have this inch?

IRAS

Not in my husband's … nose.

CHARMIAN

Heavens mend our thoughts! Alexas — come, his fortune,
his fortune. Oh Isis I implore you, let him marry a woman   50

who cannot walk, then make her die, and give him a worse
wife after that, and let worse follow worse, 'til the worst of all
follows him laughing to his grave, after she's made him fifty
times a cuckold!

IRAS

Dear goddess, hear that prayer of the people! For as it is   55
heartbreaking to see a handsome man loose-wived, so is it a
deadly sorrow to behold an ugly fellow uncuckolded.

ALEXAS

Behold! These two would turn themselves to whores if that
would give unfaithful wives to me.

Enter Cleopatra

ENOBARBUS

Hush, here comes Antony.   60

CHARMIAN

No, it's the Queen.

CLEOPATRA

Did you see my lord?

ENOBARBUS

No, lady.

CLEOPATRA

Was he not here?

CHARMIAN

No, madam.   65

CLEOPATRA

He was joyous just now, but suddenly
Was struck with Roman thoughts. Enobarbus!

ENOBARBUS

Madam?

CLEOPATRA

Seek him, and bring him here.

Exit Enobarbus

Where's Alexas? 70

ALEXAS

Here, at your service. My lord approaches.

Enter Antony with a Messenger

CLEOPATRA

I will not look upon him. Come with me.

Exit all but Antony and Messenger

MESSENGER

It was Fulvia, your wife, who waged war first.

ANTONY

Against my brother Lucius?

MESSENGER

Yes, 75

But soon that war concluded, and they merged,

And joined their forces against Caesar who,

Having the best position in the war

Drove them from Italy on first encounter.

While — 80

ANTONY

"While Antony does nothing," you would say —

MESSENGER

Oh no, my lord!

ANTONY

Speak to me plain; don't mince the public's words;

Call Cleopatra what she's called in Rome;

Lash me in Fulvia's tongue, and taunt my faults 85

With such full license as the truth allows.

Oh when our minds lie still we bring forth weeds,

And then the harshest truth will be our plowing.

Leave me alone awhile.

MESSENGER

Sir, at your pleasure. 90

8

Exit Messenger

ANTONY

I must break from these strong Egyptian chains,

Or lose myself in leisure.

Enter another Messenger with a letter

Well? What news?

3 MESSENGER

Fulvia your wife is dead.

The length of her sickness, and all other concerns   95

Important for you to know, are here.

Gives him the letter

ANTONY

Leave me.

Exit Third Messenger

There's a great spirit gone! I desired this.

What we hurl from ourselves in disesteem,

We soon will wish returned. With time's turning   100

Our present joy becomes its opposite.

She's good now, being gone. The hand that shoved

Her on now wishes it could pluck her back.

I must break free from this enchanting queen.

My sloth will hatch ten thousand greater harms   105

Than what I know already. Enobarbus!

Enter Enobarbus

ENOBARBUS

What's your pleasure, sir?

ANTONY

I must make haste from this place.

ENOBARBUS

Why then we kill our women. For unkindness is a mortal

blow to them. They could die with our departure.   110

ANTONY

I must be gone.

ENOBARBUS

Let women die for compelling reason. It is a pity to cast them
away for nothing. Cleopatra, catching wind of your departure, will die quite instantly. I have seen her die over and over
again for far lesser reasons. I do think there's a spirit in death 115
that casts a loving spell on her that she dies so readily, and
with such swiftness.

ANTONY

She is cunning beyond man's thought.

ENOBARBUS

Alas, sir, no; her passions are made of nothing but the finest
part of pure love. We cannot call her winds and waters, sighs 120
and tears; they are greater storms and tempests than alma-
nacs can report. This cannot be cunning in her.

ANTONY

If only I had never seen her!

ENOBARBUS

Oh sir, then you would have left a masterpiece unseen. You
could not call yourself a traveler. 125

ANTONY

Fulvia is dead.

ENOBARBUS

Sir?

ANTONY

Fulvia is dead.

ENOBARBUS

Fulvia?

ANTONY

Dead. 130

ENOBARBUS

Why then, give the gods a thankful sacrifice. When deities
take the wife of a man, it shows them to be true tailors of
the earth; take heart: when old robes are worn out, there's
cloth to make new clothes. If there were no more women but
Fulvia, then it would be disaster, a dark hole of lamentation. 135
But this grief is crowned with consolation; your old smock
brings forth a new petticoat, so water this sorrow with tears
of an onion.

ANTONY

The business she has thrust upon the state
Cannot endure my absence.   140

ENOBARBUS

And the business you have thrust upon here cannot be without
you, your business with Cleopatra demands that you remain.

ANTONY

No more light jesting. Let our officers
Know our intentions. I'll relay the cause
Of our expedience to Cleopatra,   145
And get her leave to part. For it is not
Fulvia's death alone that pulls me home,
But letters from our artful, scheming friends
Petition me to Rome. Sextus Pompeius
Has challenged Caesar and he now commands   150
The sea's domain. — Now his troops push forth,
Endangering the boundaries of the world.
Much peril is now breeding which can take
On sovereign life. Tell all our men that I
Require a quick remove from here.   155

ENOBARBUS

I'll do it.

Exit

ACT 1 ◆ SCENE 3

Enter Cleopatra, Charmian, Alexas, and Iras

CLEOPATRA

Where is he?

CHARMIAN

I have not seen him.

CLEOPATRA *(to Alexas)*

See where he is, who's with him, what he does.

I did not send you. If you find him sad,

Say I am dancing; if he's happy, say   5

That I'm suddenly sick. Quick, and return.

Exit Alexas

CHARMIAN

Madam, I think if you did love him dearly,

You don't pursue the proper path to make

Him feel the same.

CLEOPATRA

And what should I do different?   10

CHARMIAN

In each thing yield to him; cross him in nothing.

CLEOPATRA

You are a fool; that is the way to lose him.

CHARMIAN

Do not taunt him so far; you must refrain.

In time we hate what we too often fear.

Enter Antony

But here comes Antony.   15

CLEOPATRA

I am sick and sullen.

ANTONY

I'm sorry I must voice this present purpose —

12

CLEOPATRA

Help me away, dear Charmian! I shall fall!

The body can't sustain this torment long.

ANTONY

Now, my dearest queen —   20

CLEOPATRA

Please, stand farther from me!

ANTONY

What's the matter?

CLEOPATRA

By looking in your eyes I see good news.

What says your married woman? You may go?

If only she'd not granted you your leave!   25

Let her not say it's I that keep you here.

I have no power over you; you're hers.

ANTONY

The gods best know —

CLEOPATRA

Oh, never was there a queen

So mightily betrayed! Yet at the start   30

I saw the treasons planted.

ANTONY

Cleopatra —

CLEOPATRA

Why should I think you can be mine and true —

When you swear vows that make Olympus shake,

Yet have been false to Fulvia?   35

ANTONY

Most sweet queen —

CLEOPATRA

No, do not seek false color for your going,

Just bid farewell and go. Back when you begged

13

To stay, that was the time for lavish words:
"Eternity was in our lips and eyes, 40
Bliss in our brows; no bodily feature
Without some heavenly origin." These phrases
Must still be true, or you, the greatest soldier,
Are turned the greatest liar.

ANTONY

What is this? 45

CLEOPATRA

I wish I had your size! But you should know
There's courage in this Queen!

ANTONY

Hear me, lady.
The strong necessity of time commands
My services awhile, but my full heart 50
Remains in use with you. Our Italy
Shines with the swords of civil war; Pompeius
Makes his approaches to the port of Rome,
While our two equal factions there fight over
The pettiest details. His numbers threaten; 55
Now peace, grown sick of rest, will purge itself
With any reckless change. But my own task,
The reason you should let me go in safety,
Is Fulvia's death.

CLEOPATRA

Though age does not grant freedom from all folly, 60
It frees from childishness. Can one as great
As Fulvia really die?

ANTONY

She's dead, my queen.

(gives her the letters)

Look here, and at your leisure read of all

The turbulence she stoked. Look at the end,   65
See how she died.

CLEOPATRA

Oh most false love for her!
Where are the sacred vials that you should fill
With grave and sorrowful tears? Yes, now I see
In Fulvia's death how mine will be received.   70

ANTONY

Quarrel no more, but be prepared to learn
Of my intentions, which forever move
As you advise them. By the sun that quickens
The Nile's soil, I swear I go from here
Your soldier, servant, making peace or war   75
As you incline.

CLEOPATRA

Oh cut my bodice, Charmian, come!
So I can breathe; I swing from ill to well —
As Anthony swings his love.

ANTONY

Stop this, my queen!   80
Please see an honest love, which will sustain
An honorable test.

CLEOPATRA

So Fulvia told me
About the way you love. I urge you, turn
And weep for her. Then bid adieu to me,   85
And say her tears were really meant for me.
Play a scene of excellent dissembling
That looks like perfect honor.

ANTONY

You'll heat my blood. No more.

CLEOPATRA

You can do better yet, but this is fine.   90

ANTONY

Now by my sword —

CLEOPATRA

And your toy shield. He tries,
But this is not his best. Look, Charmian, how
This Hercules becomes the spitting image
Of an angry man.   95

ANTONY

I'll leave you, lady.

CLEOPATRA

Courteous lord, one word:
Sir, you and I must part — but that's not it;
Sir, you and I have loved — that's not it either;
These things you know — what I am trying to say —   100
My speech is lost, and I'm forgotten too.
Oh you are my oblivion!

ANTONY

If you
Were not in whole control of this display,
I'd think it real.   105

CLEOPATRA

It's like the sweating labor
Of birth to bear such nonsense in my heart
As I'm reduced to doing. But, forgive me,
Because my graces kill me when they don't
Appeal to you. Your honor calls you now;   110
Therefore be deaf to my unpitied folly,
And all the gods go with you! Upon your sword
Sit laurel victory, and smooth success
Be strewn before your feet!

ANTONY

Let us go. Come. 115

Our parting won't divide our spirit, so

That you, residing here, still travels with me,

And I, in going, still remain with you.

Away!

Exit

ACT 1 ◆ SCENE 4

Enter Octavius (Caesar) reading a letter, Lepidus, and their train

CAESAR

You must see, Lepidus, and always know,

That it is not my natural vice to hate

Our great comrade. And yet from Alexandria

This is the news: he fishes, drinks, and wastes

The lamps of night in revel; he is not 5

More manlike than Cleopatra, nor's the queen

More womanly than he; he shunned all business,

And deigned to think he had associates.

There is a man who is the sum of all

The faults that all men follow. 10

LEPIDUS

I can't think

There are enough evils to darken all

His good. His faults, in him, seem like the stars,

More fiery by night's blackness; inherent

Rather than acquired; they are what he can't change 15

Rather than what he chooses.

CAESAR

You're too indulgent. Let us grant it's not

Amiss to tumble on the bed of a queen,

To gift a kingdom for a joke, to sit

17

And keep the turns of toasting with a slave,   20
To reel the streets at noon, or to grapple
With knaves that smell of sweat. Say this becomes him —
As his character must be rare indeed
Whom these things cannot tempt — yet Antony
Cannot excuse his flaws, when we then bear   25
So great weight in his lightness. If he fills
His vacancy with his voluptuousness,
Dysentery and syphilis will claim him.
But idling away the very time
That present duty calls from us who share   30
This power jointly? *That* is to be chided.
As we admonish boys who, knowing better,
Still pawn their wisdom to their present pleasure,
Rebelling against judgment.

Enter a Messenger

LEPIDUS

Here's more news.   35

MESSENGER

Most noble Caesar, Pompey is strong
At sea and word is he's beloved by those
Who lived in fear of you. Off to the ports
The discontented hasten, and their chatter
Portray him as much wronged.   40

CAESAR

I should have seen this.

Enter another Messenger

2 MESSENGER

Caesar, I bring you word
Menecrates and Menas, infamous pirates,
Makes the sea serve them, many cruel raids
They make in Italy —   45

18

No ship peeps forth, for fear of being seen;
For Pompey's name alone can strike more blows
Than battle in the flesh could do.

CAESAR

Antony,
Leave your lascivious exploits! When you once   50
Were beaten from Modena, where you slew
Hirtius and Pansa, famine pursued you.
But you, though daintily brought up, fought hard
Against it with a mean endurance that
No savages could bear. You drank the piss   55
Of horses, and from golden puddles beasts
Would choke at. Your palate did not refuse
The roughest berry on the wildest hedge.
Yes, like the stag, when snow ensheets his pasture,
You bit the bark of trees. And on the Alps,   60
It is reported that you ate strange flesh,
Which some would die to look at. And all this —
It wounds your honor that I speak it now —
Was borne so like a soldier, not one flinch.
And so you did not starve.   65

LEPIDUS

It is a pity.

CAESAR

Let his shames quickly
Drive him to Rome. It's time the two of us
Present ourselves in the field and to that end
Immediately call a council. Pompey   70
Thrives in our idleness.
Farewell.

LEPIDUS

Farewell, my lord. What you might learn 'til then

19

Of stirrings from abroad, I do implore
You keep me well informed.   75

CAESAR

Don't doubt it, sir.

It is my bond to do just that.

Exit by different doors

ACT 1 ◆ SCENE 5

Enter Cleopatra, Charmian, Iras, and Mardian

CLEOPATRA

Charmian!

CHARMIAN

Madam?

CLEOPATRA *(yawns)*

Ah, ah.

Come let me drink of mandrake.

CHARMIAN

Why, madam?   5

CLEOPATRA

So I might sleep out this great gap of time

My Antony is away.

CHARMIAN

You think of him too much.

CLEOPATRA

That's treason!

CHARMIAN

No, Madam, it is not so.   10

CLEOPATRA

You, eunuch Mardian!

MARDIAN

What's your highness's pleasure?

CLEOPATRA

Oh, none. I take no joy in anything

A eunuch has to offer. Have you desires?

MARDIAN

Yes, gracious madam.   15

CLEOPATRA

Indeed?

MARDIAN

Not in deed, madam, for I can do nothing

But what indeed one can do, unencumbered.

Yet I have fierce desires, and think with rue

What Venus did with Mars.   20

CLEOPATRA

Oh, Charmian,

Where is he now? Does my king stand or sit?

Or does he walk? Or is he on his horse?

Oh happy horse, to bear the weight of Antony!

Go regally, horse, do you know whom you move?   25

The second Atlas of this earth, the sword

And helmet of all men! He's speaking now,

Or murmuring "Where's my serpent of old Nile?"

For so he calls me. Now I feed myself

With most delicious poison.   30

Enter Alexas from Antony

ALEXAS

Sovereign of Egypt, hail!

CLEOPATRA

How much unlike Mark Antony you are!

Yet, coming from him, by some alchemy

His gold has gilded you.

How goes it with my brave Mark Antony?   35

ALEXAS

Last thing he did, dear queen,

He kissed — the last of many doubled kisses —

This orient pearl. His speech sticks in my heart.

CLEOPATRA

My ear must pluck it from there.

ALEXAS

"Good friend," he said,   40

"Tell her this treasure of an oyster comes

From this firm Roman to the queen, and that

I will complete her opulent throne with kingdoms

To mend the petty present. Tell her all

The East shall call her mistress."   45

CLEOPATRA

What was he: sad or merry?

ALEXAS

Like to the time of year between the extremes

Of hot and cold, he was not sad nor merry.

CLEOPATRA

Oh well-divided disposition! Note him,

Good Charmian; that's just like him, just note him!   50

He was not sad, for he must cast his light

On all he leads; but neither was he merry,

Which seemed to tell them his remembrance lay

In Egypt with his joy; so he's between.

Oh heavenly mingle! Be sad or merry,   55

The violence of either becomes you

As does no other. See my messengers?

ALEXAS

Yes, twenty separate messengers. Why send

So many?

CLEOPATRA

    Whoever is born that day   60

    When I forget to message Antony

    Shall die a beggar. Ink and paper, Charmian!

    Welcome, my good Alexas! Did I, Charmian,

    Ever love Julius Caesar so?

CHARMIAN

    That splendid Julius!   65

CLEOPATRA

    Be choked with such another emphasis!

    Say, "the splendid Antony".

CHARMIAN

    The valiant Julius!

CLEOPATRA

    By Isis, I will give you bloody teeth

    If you again compare Julius to   70

    My man of men!

CHARMIAN

    By your most gracious pardon,

    I'll sing the songs you sing.

CLEOPATRA

    My salad days,

    When I was green in judgment, cold in blood,   75

    To say the things I said back then. But come,

    Get me ink and paper! He'll have greetings from

    A different messenger for every day,

    If I have to unpeople all of Egypt!

                       Exit

ACT 2 ◆ SCENE 1

Enter Pompey, Menecrates, and Menas, in warlike manner

POMPEY

If the great gods are just, they will assist

The deeds of justest men.

MENECRATES

Know, worthy Pompey,

What they delay, in time they still may grant.

POMPEY

I will do well.   5

The people love me, and the sea is mine;

My powers are budding, and my divining hope

Says they will grow to full. Mark Antony

In Egypt dines, and makes no wars outside

The bedroom walls; where Caesar gathers money   10

He loses hearts; Lepidus flatters both,

Is flattered by both; but he loves neither,

And neither cares for him.

MENAS

Caesar and Lepidus

Are in the field. They have a mighty strength.   15

POMPEY

It's false. I know they are in Rome together,

Looking for Antony. By all the charms of love,

Lewd Cleopatra, thaw your faded lip!

Let witchcraft join with beauty, lust with both;

Tie up the libertine in a field of feasts;   20

Keep his brain fuming.

Enter Varrius

What news, Varrius?

VARRIUS

    Mark Antony is due at any hour

    In Rome, and since departing from Egypt

    He has had further time for travel.   25

POMPEY

    My ear could have received any news better

    Than what you brought. Menas, I did not think

    This amorous reveler would helmet himself

    For such a petty war. His soldiership

    Is twice the other two. But let us raise   30

    A higher image of ourselves: our stirring

    Has plucked the never-lust-wearied Antony

    Straight from the lap of Egypt.

MENAS

    I can't hope

    Caesar and Antony will get on well.   35

    His wife that's dead did much offense to Caesar;

    His brother warred on him, though not, I think,

    On Antony's command.

POMPEY

    I know not, Menas,

    How lesser enmities may lead to greater.   40

    If we did not stand up against them all,

    It's clear they would have fought between themselves,

    For they have harbored causes strong enough

    To draw their swords. But how their fear of us

    May cement their divisions, and bind up   45

    Their petty differences, we don't yet know.

    Our gods decide! And for our part our lives

    Are staked on if we use our greatest strength.

    Come, Menas.

Exit

ACT 2 ◆ SCENE 2

Enter Enobarbus and Lepidus

LEPIDUS

Good Enobarbus, this cause is most worthy.

It will avail you to entreat your captain

To use his gentlest speech.

ENOBARBUS

I will entreat him

To answer as he will. If Caesar riles him,   5

Let Antony look over Caesar's head

And roar as loud as Mars.

LEPIDUS

It's not a time

For petty resentments.

ENOBARBUS

Every time   10

Must serve whatever matter that comes forth.

LEPIDUS

But smaller matters must give way to greater.

ENOBARBUS

Not if the small come first.

LEPIDUS

Your speech is passion;

I beg you, stir no embers up. Here comes   15

The noble Antony.

Enter Antony

ENOBARBUS

And there is Caesar.

Enter Caesar, Maecenas, and Agrippa

LEPIDUS

Noble friends,

The cause that had combined us was most great,

So let's not let slight actions rend us now.   20
What is amiss, may it be gently heard.
When we grow heated over minor spats,
We murder as we try to heal our wounds.

ANTONY

It's spoken well.

Flourish

CAESAR

Welcome to Rome.   25

ANTONY

Thank you.

CAESAR

Sit.

ANTONY

Sit, sir.

CAESAR

Okay then.

Caesar sits, then Antony

ANTONY

I learn you take things ill which are not so,   30
Or if they were, concern you not.

CAESAR

I must be mocked
If I should get offended over nothing,
And by you! Of all the people in the world!
More mocked still if I've spoken ill of you,   35
Invoking you if it concerned me not.

ANTONY

My being in Egypt, Caesar,
What was it to you?

CAESAR

No more than my residing here in Rome

Might be to you, in Egypt. Yet if you   40
Contrived against me here, from Egypt, I
Might be concerned.

ANTONY

How do you mean "contrived"?

CAESAR

You will soon glean at what I mean by what
Befell me here. Your wife and brother both   45
Made war upon me, and their fight was made
On your behalf; you were their word of war.

ANTONY

You have it wrong. My brother never used
Me as his cause for war. I asked and learned
About the episode from honest men   50
Who fought for you. So did my brother not
Disgrace *my* own authority with yours,
By making wars against my wishes, which
Should put the two of us in common cause?
My letters on this from before appeased,   55
So if you wish to frame a fight, I wish
It were not over this.

CAESAR

You praise yourself
By laying defects of judgment on me.
You frame your own excuses.   60
I wrote to you,
When rioting in Alexandria.
You pocketed my letters, and then jeered
My messenger out of the hall.

ANTONY

Sir,   65
He fell upon me wholly unannounced.

I'd newly feasted three kings, and was wanting
Of what I should be in the morning. But
Next day I told him of my state last night,
And asked his pardon, more or less. Let him   70
Not figure in our strife; if we contend,
Please wipe him from the ledgers.

CAESAR

You have broken
The article of your oath, a breach that you
Can never charge me with.   75

LEPIDUS

Careful, Caesar!

ANTONY

No, Lepidus, let him speak.
The honor is sacred which he talks on now,
Supposing that I lacked it. Go on, Caesar:
"The article of my oath —"   80

CAESAR

To lend me arms and aid at my request,
Both which you denied.

ANTONY

Neglected, rather,
Back then when poisoned hours had bound me up
From my own senses. As nearly as I may   85
I'll play the penitent to you, but my
Relenting will not be perceived as weak.
My honesty is my authority.
Fulvia made wars to pull me back from Egypt,
So I, the ignorant motive, do ask for   90
Sufficient pardon, as befits my honor
To stoop in such a case.

LEPIDUS

It's nobly spoken.

MAECENAS

If it might please you to enforce no further

The griefs between you; to forget them quite 95

Is to remember that the present need

Demands you three unite.

LEPIDUS

Well said, Maecenas.

ENOBARBUS

Or, if you borrow one another's love for the instant, you may,

when you hear no more words of Pompey, return it again. 100

You will have time to quarrel when you have nothing else

to do.

ANTONY

You are only a soldier. Speak no more.

ENOBARBUS

That truth should be silent, I had almost forgot.

ANTONY

You wrong this noble company; stay silent. 105

ENOBARBUS

Go on, then! Your considerate stone.

CAESAR

I don't as much dislike the matter, than

The manner of his speech; for we cannot

Remain in friendship with our characters

So differing in their acts. Yet if I knew 110

What bond would hold us tight, I would pursue

It to the edges of the earth.

AGRIPPA

Let me speak, Caesar.

CAESAR

Speak, Agrippa.

AGRIPPA   115

You have a half-sister, from your mother's side,

Admirable Octavia. Mark Antony

Is now a widower.

CAESAR

Say not so, Agrippa.

If Cleopatra heard you, you'd deserve   120

A reproof for your rashness.

ANTONY

I am not married, Caesar. Let me hear

Agrippa speak further.

AGRIPPA

To hold you in perpetual good standing,

To make you brothers, and to knit your hearts   125

With an unslipping knot, let Antony wed

Your fair Octavia, whose beauty calls

For no less than the best of men to marry.

Whose virtues and whose general graces speak

What no mortal can utter. By this marriage   130

All small suspicions which now seem so great,

And all great fears which carry greater dangers,

Would then be nothing. Most unpleasant truths

Would quiet to mere gossip, just as gossip

Now shouts as loudest truth. Her love to both   135

Would bind you, and all loves that follow you

Would bind together in her.

ANTONY

Will Caesar speak?

CAESAR

Not till he hears how Antony is touched

32

By what is spoke already.   140

ANTONY

What power is in Agrippa,

If I would say "Agrippa, make it so,"

To make this good?

CAESAR

The power of Caesar, and

His power over Octavia.   145

ANTONY

To this good plan

So fairly put forth thus, let me never

Dream of impediment! Let me have your hand.

Let us dispatch this act of grace, and from

This hour the heart of brothers lead our loves   150

And sway our great designs!

CAESAR

There's my hand.

(they clasp hands)

A sister I bequeath you, whom no brother

Did ever love so dearly. Let her live

To join our kingdoms and our hearts; and ensure   155

Our love never again flies off!

LEPIDUS

Amen!

ANTONY

I did not think I'd draw my sword on Pompey,

For he of late has laid strange courtesies

Upon me. I must thank him, only so   160

My honor does not suffer ill report;

But after that, defy him.

LEPIDUS

Time calls us.

We must seek out Pompey with greatest haste
Or he will seek us first.   165

ANTONY

What is his strength by land?

CAESAR

Great and increasing, but by sea
He is an absolute master.

ANTONY

So is the report.
If only we'd met sooner! Let's make haste.   170
Before we put ourselves in arms, let's seal
This business we have talked of.

CAESAR

With most gladness,
I do invite you to behold my sister.
I'll lead you to her.   175

ANTONY

Lepidus, let's not lack your company.

LEPIDUS

Noble Antony, no sickness would detain me.

Flourish

Exit all except Enobarbus, Agrippa, and Maecenas

MAECENAS

Welcome from Egypt, sir.

ENOBARBUS

Half the heart of Caesar, worthy Maecenas! My honorable
friend, Agrippa!   180

AGRIPPA

Good Enobarbus!

MAECENAS

We have cause to be glad that matters are so well settled. You
stood up well in Egypt.

ACT 2 ◆ SCENE 2

ENOBARBUS

    Yes, sir, we disoriented the day by sleeping through it, and

    making the night light with drinking.   185

MAECENAS

    She's a most triumphant lady, if reports are honest to her.

ENOBARBUS

    When she first met Mark Antony, she pocketed up his heart

    upon the river of Cydnus.

AGRIPPA

    She indeed appeared there. Or my reporter devised good story

    for her.   190

ENOBARBUS

    I will tell you.

    The barge she sat in, like a burnished throne

    Burned on the water; the stern was beaten gold;

    The sails were purple; and so perfumed that

    The winds were love-sick with them; the oars were silver, 195

    Which to the tune of flutes kept stroke, and made

    The water which they beat flow faster,

    Amorous of their strokes. For her own person,

    It defied any description; for she lay

    In her pavilion, clothed in gold weaving,   200

    Out-picturing that portrait of Venus where

    The artist outworks nature. By her sides

    Stood pretty dimpled boys, like smiling cupids,

    With different-colored fans, whose wind did seem

    To make their tender cheeks glow red, heating 205

    The very thing they cooled.

AGRIPPA

    How magical for Antony!

ENOBARBUS

    Her gentlewomen, like the sea king's daughters,

35

So many mermaids, tended her with eyes,
Adorning her with gazes. At the helm   210
A seeming mermaid steers. The silken sail
Swells with the touches of those flower-soft hands
That do their task with deftness. From the barge
A strange invisible perfume hits the senses
Of the adjacent shores. The city cast   215
Her people out upon her, and Antony,
Enthroned within the marketplace, sat whistling
Into the air; if air could leave without
Making a gap in nature, it would too
Have gone to gaze on Cleopatra.   220

AGRIPPA

Magical Egyptian!

ENOBARBUS

Upon her landing, Antony sent for her;
Invited her to supper. She replied
It would be better if he was *her* guest,
Which she insisted. Our courteous Antony,   225
Of whom a woman's never heard a "no,"
Being barbered ten times over, goes to feast,
And, for his supper, filled only his heart;
He ate with his eyes only.

AGRIPPA

Royal wench!   230
She made great Julius lay his sword to bed.
He plowed her, she bore fruit.

ENOBARBUS

I saw her once
Hop forty paces through the public street,
And, though she lost her breath, still spoke and panted.   235
She turned her defect into perfection;

Breathless, she poured breath forth.

MAECENAS

Now Antony must leave her utterly.

ENOBARBUS

Never! He will not.

Age cannot wither her, nor custom stale   240

Her infinite variety. Some women fill

The appetites they feed, but she makes hungry

Where she most satisfies; for vilest things

In her become becoming; holy priests

Bless her when she most sins.   245

MAECENAS

If beauty, wisdom, modesty can settle

The heart of Antony, Octavia is

A blessed lottery to him.

Exit

ACT 2 ◆ SCENE 3

Enter Antony, Caesar; Octavia between them

ANTONY

The world and my great office will sometimes

Divide me from your bosom.

OCTAVIA

At which time

When I should bend my knees before the gods,

My prayers will bend to you.   5

ANTONY

My Octavia

Do not read of my flaws in the world's report.

I've strayed outside the grid, but what's come

Will keep inside the lines. Good night, dear lady.

Sir.   10

OCTAVIA

Good night, sir.

CAESAR

Good night.

Exit Caesar and Octavia

Enter Soothsayer

ANTONY

My man! Do you wish you were back in Egypt?

SOOTHSAYER

Had I not come from there, and you not gone!

ANTONY

What do you mean by that? 15

SOOTHSAYER

I see things in my mind that lack clear meaning.

But you must leave again for Egypt.

ANTONY

Tell me

Whose fortunes will rise higher, Caesar's or mine?

SOOTHSAYER

Caesar's. 20

Therefore, do not stay by his side, oh Antony.

Your soul — Your very spirit that lives in you —

Is noble, brave, unmatched by none. But only

When Caesar is away. Near him, your soul

Becomes afraid, as if it's overpowered. 25

Therefore make space between you.

ANTONY

Speak no more.

SOOTHSAYER

I'll speak no more except to you alone.

If you should play with him at any game,

You're sure to lose; he beats you against all 30

The odds in natural luck. Your splendor dims
When he shines by. I say again, your spirit
Is all afraid to govern you near him;
It's noble when he's far.

ANTONY

Be gone with you.   35

Exit Soothsayer

By skill or chance the soothsayer speaks true.
The very dice obey the young Caesar.
And in our sports my better prowess faints
Under his chance. If we draw lots, he wins;
His cocks best mine in battle every time.   40
Even when I have odds, his quails will win
When put into the ring. I'll leave to Egypt;
Though I must make this marriage for our peace,
My pleasure lies in the East.

Exit

ACT 2 ◆ SCENE 4

Enter Cleopatra, Charmian, Iras, and Alexas

CLEOPATRA

Give me some music — melancholy food
For us that trade in love.

ALL

The music, play!

Enter Mardian the Eunuch

CLEOPATRA

Leave it alone. Let's do billiards. Come, Charmian.

CHARMIAN

My arm is sore. Best play with Mardian.   5

CLEOPATRA

A woman plays with eunuchs as she'd play

With other women. Come, you'll play with me, sir?

MARDIAN

As well as I can play.

CLEOPATRA

And when good will is shown, the actor may
Plead pardon if his skill cuts short. No billiards.　　　10
My fishing rod! We'll go down to the river.
There, with my music playing, I'll entrap
Its dark-finned fishes. My bended hook will pierce
Their slimy jaws, and, as I draw them up,
I'll think of every one an Antony,　　　15
And say "Ah, ha! You're caught!"

CHARMIAN

That time you bet
Him on your fishing, then your diver hung
A salt-cured fish upon his hook, which he
With fervency drew up.　　　20

CLEOPATRA

That time? Oh times!
I laughed him out of patience, and that night
I laughed him into patience, and next day,
At nine o'clock, I drunk him to his bed,
Then put my cloak and head-dress on him, while　　　25
I wore his sword.

Enter a Messenger

Oh, news from Italy!
Come ram your fruitful tidings in my ears,
That have been barren for so long!

MESSENGER

Madam —　　　30

CLEOPATRA

My Antony's dead! If you say so, villain,

40

You kill your mistress; but if you report
Him well and free, there will be gold, and here
My bluest veins to kiss, a hand that kings
Have lipped like lap dogs, trembling while they kissed.   35

MESSENGER

First, madam, he is well.

CLEOPATRA

Well, there's more gold.
But please note, my good man: we often say
The dead are well. If that is what you mean
I'll melt the gold I give you, and will pour   40
It down your ill-uttering throat.

MESSENGER

Good madam, hear me —

CLEOPATRA

I will you, please go on.
Yet if Antony's free and healthful I
Don't see this in your face. So sour a face   45
To trumpet such good news! And if he's ill,
You should come like a Fury crowned with snakes,
Not like a normal man.

MESSENGER

Will it please you to hear me?

CLEOPATRA

I want to strike you down before you speak.   50
Yet if you say Antony lives, is well,
Or friends with Caesar, and not captive to him,
I'll set you in a shower of gold and hail
Rich pearls upon you.

MESSENGER

Madam, he's well.   55

CLEOPATRA

Well said!

MESSENGER

And friends with Caesar.

CLEOPATRA

You're a worthy man!

MESSENGER

Caesar and he are greater friends than ever.

CLEOPATRA

You've made a fortune from me! 60

MESSENGER

But yet, madam —

CLEOPATRA

I do not like "But yet". It does dispel

The good that came before. I curse "But yet"!

"But yet" is as a jailer bringing forth

Some monstrous malefactor. Please you, friend, 65

Unpack your peddler's wares into my ear,

The good and bad together. He's friends with Caesar,

In a good state of health, and you say, free.

MESSENGER

Free, madam? No, I made no such report.

He is bound to Octavia. 70

CLEOPATRA

In what way?

MESSENGER

To have their way in bed.

CLEOPATRA

I'm pale, Charmian.

MESSENGER

Madam, he's married to Octavia.

CLEOPATRA

The most infectious pestilence upon you!   75

Strikes him down

MESSENGER

Good madam, patience!

CLEOPATRA

What did you say?

(strikes him)

Away,

Horrible villain, or I'll kick your eyes

Like balls before me. I'll unhair your head!   80

(she drags him around the stage)

You will be whipped with wire and stewed in brine,

Burning in lingering pickle!

MESSENGER

Gracious madam,

I bring the news but did not make the match.

CLEOPATRA

Say it's not so, and I'll give you a province,   85

And make your fortunes great.

MESSENGER

He's married, madam.

CLEOPATRA

Rogue, you have lived too long!

Draws a knife

MESSENGER

Okay, I'll run.

Madame, what is this? I have made no fault.   90

Exit

CHARMIAN

Good madam, keep yourself within yourself.

The man is innocent.

CLEOPATRA

Some innocents do not escape the lightning.

Melt Egypt into Nile, and kindly creatures

All turn to serpents! Call the slave again!   95

Though I am mad, I will not bite him. Call!

CHARMIAN

He is afraid to come.

CLEOPATRA

I will not hurt him.

Exit Charmian

These hands lack nobleness when they should strike

A lesser than myself, especially   100

Since I myself have worked myself to rage.

Enter the Messenger again with Charmian

Come here, sir.

Though it is honest, it is never easy

To bring bad news.

MESSENGER

I've done my duty.   105

CLEOPATRA

Is he married?

I cannot hate you worser than I do

If you again say "Yes".

MESSENGER

He's married, madam.

CLEOPATRA

The gods destroy you! Do you still say that?   110

MESSENGER

Should I lie?

CLEOPATRA

Yes! Even if in so doing

The gods drowned half my Egypt, turning it

Into a cistern for scaled snakes. Get gone!

If you had the fair face of Narcissus,   115

You'd still be ugly to me. He is married?

MESSENGER

I crave your highness's pardon.

CLEOPATRA

He is married?

MESSENGER

Take no offense, I don't wish to offend you.

To punish me for what you make me do   120

Seems most unfair. He's married to Octavia.

CLEOPATRA

Oh, that his fault should make a rogue of you

Who hurts without his knowledge! Get away!

Exit Messenger

CHARMIAN

Madam, patience.

CLEOPATRA

In loving Antony, I have unloved Caesar.   125

CHARMIAN

Many times, Queen.

CLEOPATRA

I will pay for it now.

Lead me from here;

I faint! Oh Iras, Charmian! I'm fine.

Go to the fellow, good Alexas, bid him   130

Report to me Octavia's features, tell me

Her temperament, her years, do not leave out

The color of her hair. Bring me word quickly.

Exit Alexas

Let Antony be banished! Let him not.

From certain angles he is like a Gorgon,   135

45

From other views, a Mars.

(to Iras)

    Go bid Alexas

Bring me word how tall she is. Pity me, Charmian,

But do not speak to me. Lead me to my chamber.

Exit

ACT 2 ◆ SCENE 5

Flourish

Enter Pompey and Menas at one door with drum and trumpet;
at another, Caesar, Lepidus, Antony, Enobarbus, Maecenas,
Agrippa, with Soldiers marching

POMPEY

You have my hostages and I have yours.

Let's talk before we fight.

CAESAR

    Tradition says

That first we should try words. Therefore we've sent

Our written propositions to you first.   5

POMPEY

To you all three,

Sole senators alone of this great world,

Chief agents for the gods: I do not think

My father lacks in agents for revenge,

Having a son and friends; like Julius Caesar,   10

Who as a ghost visited good Brutus,

Had *you* to strive for him when he was killed.

But what had moved pale Cassius to conspire?

Or the honest Roman, Brutus, with his partners,

Courtiers of beauteous freedom, go and drench   15

The Capitol in blood, but to proclaim

A man is but a man, and must be stopped

46

If he is raised above us as a god?
And this is why I rig my navy, at
Whose load the angered ocean foams. I mean   20
To scourge the disrespect that hateful Rome
Cast on my noble father.

CAESAR

Settle down.

ANTONY

You cannot scare us with your sails, Pompey.
We'll speak with you at sea. On land you know   25
By how much we outnumber you.

POMPEY

On land
You outmatched me of my own father's house,
But since the cuckoo takes but cannot build,
Remain there while you can.   30

LEPIDUS

These matters aren't
Priority. Please tell us how you take
The offers we have sent you.

CAESAR

There's the point.

POMPEY

You've made to me the offer   35
Of Sicily, Sardinia; and I must
Rid all the sea of pirates; and then send
Measures of wheat to Rome. This deal approved,
We part our separate ways with unhacked blades,
Our shields undented.   40

CAESAR, ANTONY, LEPIDUS

That's our offer.

POMPEY

    Know, then,

    I came before you here a man prepared

    To take this offer, but Mark Antony

    Put me to some impatience. Though I lose   45

    The praise of it by telling, you must know

    When Caesar and your brother were at blows,

    Your mother came to Sicily and found

    A friendly welcome.

ANTONY

    So I've heard, Pompey,   50

    And come prepared to give the liberal thanks

    I owe to you.

POMPEY

    Then let me have your hand.

(they shake hands)

    I did not think, sir, to have met you here.

ANTONY

    The beds in the East are far too soft; I thank you,   55

    Who called me here much sooner than intended.

    For I have gained by it.

LEPIDUS

    That's well said for us all!

POMPEY

    I hope so, Lepidus. So we're agreed.

    I want for our arrangement to be written   60

    And sealed between us.

CAESAR

    That's the next to do.

POMPEY

    Let's have a round of feasts! We can draw lots

    To see who plays host first.

ANTONY

    I'll host the first! 65

POMPEY

    No, Antony, take the lot.

    But, first or last, your fine Egyptian cookery

    Will have the fame. I have heard that Julius Caesar

    Grew fat with feasting there.

ANTONY

    You have heard much. 70

POMPEY

    I have good meanings, sir.

ANTONY

    And good words for them.

POMPEY

    Then I have heard so much.

    Like I've heard Julius's servant carried —

ENOBARBUS

    No more of that! He did so. 75

POMPEY

    What, please tell?

ENOBARBUS

    Carry a queen to Caesar in a mattress.

POMPEY

    We're friends now. How do you fare, soldier?

ENOBARBUS

    Well;

    And well in times to come for I perceive 80

    Four feasts are imminent.

POMPEY

    I'll shake your hand.

(they shake hands)

    I never hated you. I've seen you fight

And I have envied your behavior.

ENOBARBUS

Sir,   85

I never loved you much, but have praised you

When you have well deserved ten times as much

As I have said you did.

POMPEY

Enjoy your plainness;

It doesn't do you ill.   90

I now invite you all aboard my galley.

Will you lead, lords?

CAESAR, ANTONY, LEPIDUS

Show us the way, sir.

POMPEY

Come.

Exit all but Enobarbus and Menas

MENAS *(aside)*

Your father, Pompey, would never have made this treaty.   95

(to Enobarbus)

You and I have met, sir.

ENOBARBUS

At sea, I think.

MENAS

We have, sir.

ENOBARBUS

You have done well by water.

MENAS

And you by land.   100

ENOBARBUS

I will praise any man that will praise me, though it cannot be
denied what I have done by land.

MENAS

Nor what I have done by water.

ENOBARBUS

Perhaps you should deny this for your safety: you have been
a great thief by sea.   105

MENAS

And you by land.

ENOBARBUS

Then I deny my land service. But give me your hand, Menas!

(they shake hands)

We came here to fight with you.

MENAS

For my part, I am sorry it is turned to drinking. This day
Pompey laughs away his fortune.   110

ENOBARBUS

If he does, he surely cannot weep it back again.

MENAS

Quite right, sir. We did not think Mark Antony would be
here. Tell me, is he married to Cleopatra?

ENOBARBUS

Caesar's sister is called Octavia.

MENAS

True, sir. She was the wife of Caius Marcellus.   115

ENOBARBUS

But she is now the wife of Marcus Antonius.

MENAS

I beg your pardon, sir?

ENOBARBUS

It's true.

MENAS

Then Caesar and he are forever knit together.

ENOBARBUS

But If I were forced to divine this unity, I would not proph- 120
esy it's future. I think you will find the band that seems to
tie their friendship together will be the very strangler of it.
Octavia is of a holy, cold, and meek disposition.

MENAS

Who would not have his wife so?

ENOBARBUS

Not he who is not so himself; which Antony is not. He'll go to 125
his Egyptian dish again. Antony will turn his affection where
he wants. He married but necessity here.

MENAS

And so it may be. Come, sir, will you board? I have a drink
for you.

ENOBARBUS

I will take it, sir. We have trained our throats in Egypt. 130

Exit

ACT 2 ◆ SCENE 6

A trumpet sounded

*Enter Caesar, Antony, Pompey, Lepidus, Agrippa, Maecenas,
Enobarbus, and Menas, with other captains*

ANTONY

They do it thus: take measure of the Nile
By certain scales within the pyramid.
They know by where the water sits if dearth
Or plenty follow. Higher swells the Nile,
The more it promises. 5

LEPIDUS

You've strange serpents there?

ANTONY

Yes, Lepidus.

LEPIDUS

Your serpent of Egypt is bred from your mud, by the operation of your sun; so is your crocodile.

ANTONY

They are so.   10

POMPEY

Sit, and drink more wine! A health to Lepidus!

They sit and drink

LEPIDUS

I am not as well as I should be, but I'll never say no.

ENOBARBUS *(aside)*

Not till you pass out. I fear you'll be a yes 'til then.

LEPIDUS

No, certainly, I have heard the Ptolemies' pyramids are quite
amazing things. Without contradiction I have heard that.   15

MENAS *(aside to Pompey)*

Pompey, a word.

POMPEY *(aside to Menas)*

Leave me alone for now — This wine for Lepidus!

LEPIDUS

What manner of thing is your crocodile?

ANTONY

It is shaped, sir, like itself, and it is as broad as it has breadth.
It is just so high as it is, and moves with its own organs. It   20
lives by that which nourishes it, and once the elements are
out of it, it transmigrates.

LEPIDUS

What color is it of?

ANTONY

Of it own color, too.

LEPIDUS

'Tis a strange serpent.   25

ANTONY

'Tis so, and the tears of it are wet.

CAESAR

Will this description satisfy him?

ANTONY

He should be satisfied with what he's drank.

POMPEY *(aside to Menas)*

Go hang, sir, hang! Tell me of what? Away,

Do as I bid you. — Where's this cup I called for? 30

MENAS *(aside to Pompey)*

In the name of all my service, you will hear me,

Rise from your stool.

POMPEY *(aside to Menas)*

I think you're mad. What is it?

Rises and walks with Menas

MENAS

I've always bowed my head to your fortunes.

POMPEY

You've served me with much faith. What else to say? — 35

Be jolly, lords.

ANTONY

These quicksands, Lepidus,

Keep off them, for you sink.

MENAS

Will you be lord of all the world?

POMPEY

What are you saying? 40

MENAS

I'll say again: Will you be lord of all

The world?

POMPEY

How could that be?

MENAS

    If you want it,

    Then I, though I am poor, will be the man   45

    Who gives you all the world.

POMPEY

    Have you drunk well?

MENAS

    No, Pompey, I have kept myself from drink.

    These three world-sharers, these competitors,

    Are in your vessel. Let me cut the cable,   50

    And when we are adrift, I'll slit their throats.

    Then all is yours.

POMPEY

    Ah, this you should have done

    Without speaking. For me, it's villainy;

    For you it would had been good service.   55

    For done unknown,

    I would have found it afterwards well done,

    But must condemn it now. Desist and drink.

Returns to the others

MENAS *(aside)*

    For this,

    I won't follow your feebled fortunes more.   60

    For he who seeks and will not take when offered,

    Will never find again.

POMPEY

    This health to Lepidus!

ANTONY

    Bear him ashore. I'll drink for him, Pompey.

ENOBARBUS

    Here's to you, Menas!   65

MENAS

Enobarbus, welcome!

POMPEY

Fill till the cup be hid.

ENOBARBUS *(points to the Attendant who carries off Lepidus)*

There's a strong fellow, Menas.

MENAS

Why?

ENOBARBUS

He bears the third part of the world, man. See?   70

MENAS

The third part then is drunk. Were it all three,

The world would spin on wheels!

ENOBARBUS

Drink you!

POMPEY

This is not yet an Alexandrian feast.

ANTONY

It ripens towards it. Strike the vessels, come!   75

Here's to Caesar!

CAESAR

I should well forbear it.

It's monstrous labor when I wash my brain

And it grows fouler.

ANTONY

Be a child of the time.   80

CAESAR

"Possess it," is my answer.

I'd rather fast from everything, four days,

Than drink that much in one.

ENOBARBUS *(to Antony)*

Ha, my brave Emperor,

Shall we dance now the Egyptian Bacchanals 85
And celebrate our drink?

CAESAR

What more? Pompey, good night. Brother let me
Request you on the shore. Our graver business
Frowns at this levity. Gentle lords, let's part.
You see we have burnt our cheeks. Strong Enobarb 90
Is weaker than the wine, and my own tongue
Splits what it speaks. The masquerade has almost
Grotesqued us all. What words are left? Good night.
Good Antony, your hand.

Exit

ACT 3 ◆ SCENE 1

Enter Agrippa at one door, Enobarbus at another

AGRIPPA

What, have our three leaders gone already?

ENOBARBUS

They've settled with Pompey, who's gone. The rest
Are now signing their deal. Octavia weeps
To part from Rome; Caesar is sad, and Lepidus
Since Pompey's feast, as Menas says, is troubled   5
With the green-sickness.

AGRIPPA

He's noble, that Lepidus.

ENOBARBUS

He leapt-at-us with fineness. How he loves Caesar!

AGRIPPA

No, but how dearly he adores Mark Antony!

ENOBARBUS

"Caesar? Why, he's the Jupiter of men!"   10

AGRIPPA

"What's Antony? The god of Jupiter!"

ENOBARBUS

"You spoke of Caesar? Hoo! The incomparable!"

AGRIPPA

"Oh Antony! You rare Arabian bird!"

ENOBARBUS

"To praise Caesar, say 'Caesar.' Go no further."

AGRIPPA

Indeed, that Lepidus plied both with excellent praises.   15

ENOBARBUS

But he loves Caesar best. Yet he loves Antony.

AGRIPPA

He loves both.

ENOBARBUS

They are his dung and he their beetle.

Trumpet within

Enter Caesar, Antony, Lepidus, and Octavia

ANTONY

I've heard your points, no more.

CAESAR

You take from me a great part of myself.   20

So treat me well. Sister, prove such a wife

As my thoughts make you, so my every word

May be pledged on your conduct. Noble Antony,

Do not allow this piece of virtue set

Between us, as the cement of our love,   25

Become the ram to batter it instead.

For we must love her equally, or else

Look for a different broker.

ANTONY

Don't offend me

With your distrust.   30

CAESAR

I've made my point.

ANTONY

You will not find,

Though you are dubious, the least cause

For what you seem to fear. The gods protect you,

And make the hearts of Romans serve your ends.   35

Here we part.

CAESAR

    Farewell, my dearest sister, fare you well.

    The seasons be most kind to you, and make

    Your spirits all of comfort! Fare you well.

OCTAVIA

    My noble brother!   40

She weeps

ANTONY

    It's April in her eyes; it is love's spring.

    Yet showers bring the blooms of May. Be cheerful.

OCTAVIA *(to Caesar)*

    Sir please look kindly to my husband's house, and —

CAESAR

    What, Octavia?

OCTAVIA

    I'll tell you in your ear.   45

She whispers to Caesar

ANTONY

    Her tongue does not express her heart, but then

    Her heart does not direct the tongue. She is

    A feather sitting still upon the swell

    Of tide, neither way inclining.

ENOBARBUS *(aside to Agrippa)*

    Is Caesar about to weep?   50

AGRIPPA *(aside to Enobarbus)*

    Why, Enobarbus,

    When Antony found Julius Caesar dead,

    He cried almost to roaring, and he wept

    At Philippi when he found Brutus slain.

ENOBARBUS *(aside to Agrippa)*

    That year he was accursed with watery eyes.   55

CAESAR

No, sweet Octavia, you'll hear from me often.

A minute will not pass without my thoughts

Directed toward you.

ANTONY

Come, sir, come.

I'll wrestle with you in my strength of love. 60

Look, here I have you *(embracing him)*; now I let you go,

And give you to the gods.

CAESAR

Adieu. Be happy!

LEPIDUS

Let all the number of the stars give light

To your fair way! 65

CAESAR

Farewell, farewell!

Kisses Octavia

ANTONY

Farewell!

Trumpets sound

Exit

ACT 3 ◆ SCENE 2

Enter Cleopatra, Charmian, Iras, and Alexas

CLEOPATRA

Where is that messenger?

ALEXAS

Afraid to come.

CLEOPATRA

Go to, go to.

Enter the Messenger as before

Come here, sir.

Come closer! 5

MESSENGER

Most gracious majesty!

CLEOPATRA

Did you behold

Octavia?

MESSENGER

Ay, dread Queen.

CLEOPATRA

Where? 10

MESSENGER

Madam, in Rome.

I looked her in the face, and saw her led

Between her brother and Mark Antony.

CLEOPATRA

Is she as tall as me?

MESSENGER

She is not, madam. 15

CLEOPATRA

Did you hear her speak? Is she shrill-tongued or low?

MESSENGER

Madam, I heard her speak; she is low-voiced.

CLEOPATRA

That's not so good. He cannot like her long.

CHARMIAN

Like her? Oh Isis! It's impossible.

CLEOPATRA

I think so, Charmian. Dull of tongue and dwarfish. 20

What majesty is in her walk? Remember,

If ever you looked on majesty.

MESSENGER

She creeps.

Her movement is as though she's standing still.
She shows a body rather than a soul, 25
A statue than a breather.

CLEOPATRA

Is this certain?

MESSENGER

Or I cannot observe.

CHARMIAN

Three Egyptians
Could not observe her better. 30

CLEOPATRA

He can see.
I do perceive. There's nothing in her yet.
The fellow has good judgment.

CHARMIAN

Very good.

CLEOPATRA

Guess at her years, I beg you. 35

MESSENGER

Madam,
She is a widow —

CLEOPATRA

Widow? Charmian, listen!

MESSENGER

And I do think she's thirty.

CLEOPATRA

Do you recall her face? Is it long or round? 40

MESSENGER

Round, even to faultiness.

CLEOPATRA

The round-faced folks are often foolish too.
Her hair, what color?

MESSENGER

    Brown, madam, and her forehead:

    She would not want it lower.   45

CLEOPATRA

    There's gold for you.

    You must not take my former sharpness ill.

    I will employ you back again; I find you

    Most fit for business. Go, and get ready;

    Our letters are prepared.   50

Exit Messenger

CHARMIAN

    A fine man.

CLEOPATRA

    Indeed, he is so. I do much repent

    That I so frighted him. I think, from him,

    This creature's nothing special.

CHARMIAN

    Nothing, madam.   55

CLEOPATRA

    The man has seen some majesty, and should know.

CHARMIAN

    Has he seen majesty? By Isis, yes!

    From serving you so long!

CLEOPATRA

    I have one thing more to ask him yet, good Charmian.

    But it's no matter; you will bring him to me   60

    Where I will write. All may be well enough.

Exit

ACT 3 ♦ SCENE 3

Enter Antony and Octavia

ANTONY

No, no, Octavia, not only that.

That, on its own, could be excusable.

That and a thousand more — for he has waged

New wars against Pompey; he read his will

In public, to seem generous; then he   5

Spoke grudgingly of me, and when called on

To pay me terms of praise, he vented them

Sickly and cold; the smallest measure lent me;

When any chance arose to credit me,

He did not bite, or spoke through gritted teeth.   10

OCTAVIA

Oh, my good lord,

Believe not all, or if you must believe,

Resent not all. If rifts befall you two,

A more sad lady never stood between,

Praying for both parts.   15

The good gods will mock me at once,

When I should pray: "Oh, bless my lord and husband!";

And then undo that prayer by crying out

"Oh, bless my brother!" "Husband win!" "Win brother!"

My prayers destroy the prayer; no midway   20

Between extremes.

ANTONY

Gentle Octavia, let

Your spirit guide you to the one who seeks

Best to preserve it. If I lose my honor,

I lose myself; then best I were not yours   25

Than yours so stripped. As you requested, you

Will mediate. But in the meantime, lady,

66

I'll raise the preparation of a war
That stains your brother. Make your soonest haste,
If that is your desire.   30

OCTAVIA

Thanks to my lord.
The might of all the gods makes me, most weak,
Your reconciler! Wars between you two
Would make the world cleave open, and slain men
Would fill the chasm.   35

ANTONY

When it is clear to you who started this,
Turn your displeasure that way, for our faults
Can never be so equal that your love
Can move between them equally. Prepare
Your going. Choose your company, and ask   40
Whatever cost your heart desires.

Exit

ACT 3 ◆ SCENE 4

Enter Enobarbus and Eros, meeting

ENOBARBUS

How goes it now, friend Eros?

EROS

There's strange news coming, sir.

ENOBARBUS

What, man?

EROS

Caesar and Lepidus have made wars upon Pompey.

ENOBARBUS

This is old. What is the outcome?   5

EROS

Caesar, having made use of Lepidus in the wars against Pompey,

at once denied his equal standing; would not let him partake
in the glory of the action, and, not stopping here, accuses
him of treason, from letters Lepidus wrote to Pompey long
ago; then, on pretense of his own invented charges, Caesar 10
seizes him. So poor Lepidus is imprisoned, till death enlarge
his confine.

ENOBARBUS

Then, world, you have but two jaws left remaining.
And throw between them all the food you have,
They'll grind each other down. Where's Antony? 15

EROS

He's walking in the garden, kicking, thus,
The grass before him; cries "Fool Lepidus!",
And threatens the throat of his own officer
Who murdered Pompey.

ENOBARBUS

Our great navy's readied. 20

EROS

For Italy and Caesar. More, Enobarbus:
My lord desires you promptly. I should have
Told you of this before my news.

ENOBARBUS

Don't worry.
It won't be anything. Bring me to Antony. 25

EROS

Come, sir.

Exit

ACT 3 ◆ SCENE 5

Enter Agrippa, Maecenas, and Caesar

CAESAR

Contempting Rome, he's done all this, and more

In Alexandria. Here's the sum of it:
In the marketplace, on a tribunal stage,
Cleopatra and himself in chairs of gold
Were publicly enthroned. At their feet sat   5
Caesarion, whom they call my father's son,
And all the unlawful urchins that their lust
Since then has made between them. Unto her
He affirmed her claim of Egypt; then made her
Absolute Queen of lower Syria,   10
Cyprus, Lydia.

MAECENAS

This in the public eye?

CAESAR

In the common showplace, where they exercise. Cleopatra
That day appeared dressed as the goddess Isis
And gave free audience to her subjects,   15
As it's reported, so.

MAECENAS

Relay this to the Roman people.

AGRIPPA

Who, queasy with his insolence already,
Will banish every last good thought of him.

CAESAR

The people know it, and have now received   20
His accusations.

AGRIPPA

Who does he accuse?

CAESAR

Me! Saying that, after plundering Pompey
In Sicily, I had not portioned him
His share. He then says I have not returned   25
Some ships he lent to me. Lastly, he frets

That we had deposed Lepidus at all!
And having done so, that we should detain
All of his revenue.

AGRIPPA

This should be answered. 30

CAESAR

It's done already, and the messenger sent.
I've told Antony that Lepidus grew cruel,
That he abused his high authority
And did deserve his fate. For what I conquered,
I grant him part; but then in his Armenia, 35
And other parts of all his conquered kingdoms,
I demand the same.

MAECENAS

He'll never yield to that.

CAESAR

Nor will we yield to him in his demands.

Enter Octavia with her train

OCTAVIA

Hail, Caesar, my lord! Hail, my most dear Caesar! 40

CAESAR

That I should ever call you castaway!

OCTAVIA

You have not called me so, nor have you cause.

CAESAR

Why have you stolen here like this? You don't come
Like Caesar's sister. The wife of Antony
Should have an army for an usher, and 45
The neighs of horses blasting her approach
Before she can be seen. But here you come
A market maid to Rome, and have prevented
The ostentation of my love which, left unshown,

70

Is often left unfelt.   50

OCTAVIA

My lord,

I was not forced to come like this, it was

On my free will. My lord, Mark Antony,

Hearing that you prepared for war, acquainted

My weeping ear with this, whereon I begged   55

His consent to return.

CAESAR

Which he fast granted,

Since you are an obstruction to his lust.

OCTAVIA

Do not say so, my lord.

CAESAR

I have eyes upon him,   60

And his affairs come to me on the wind.

Where is he now?

OCTAVIA

My lord, in Athens.

CAESAR

No,

My most wronged sister. Cleopatra has   65

Nodded him to her. He has given his empire

Up to a whore, and they now are gathering

The kings of the earth for war.

OCTAVIA

Oh me, most wretched,

Whose heart is split apart between two friends   70

Who do afflict each other!

CAESAR

You're home now.

Your letters did forestall my battle plans.

But now I see both how you were misled
And how I am at risk through negligence. 75
Be cheered. Welcome
To Rome, my dearest one! You are deceived
Beyond the boundary of thought, the gods
Make us, and those you love, their ministers,
For we will do you justice. Be in comfort. 80
You're always welcome to me.

AGRIPPA

Welcome, lady.

MAECENAS

Welcome, dear madam.
Each heart in Rome does love and pity you.
Only adulterous Antony, most large 85
In his abominations, turns you out
And cedes his potent power to a whore
That noises it against us.

OCTAVIA

Is it so, sir?

CAESAR

Most certain. Sister, welcome. I beseech you, 90
Continue to be patient. Dearest sister!

Exit

ACT 3 ◆ SCENE 6

Enter Cleopatra and Enobarbus

CLEOPATRA

I will get even with you, don't doubt it.

ENOBARBUS

But why, why, why?

CLEOPATRA

You spoke against my being in these wars;

You said it is not fit.

ENOBARBUS

Well, is it, is it?   5

CLEOPATRA

This war's declared upon me too. Why should

I not be there in person?

ENOBARBUS

Your presence will distract poor Antony,

You'd borrow from his heart and brain and time

What can't be spared. He is already blamed   10

For levity; and it is said in Rome

That Photinus, a eunuch, and your maids

Manage this war.

CLEOPATRA

Sink Rome, and let those tongues

Who speak against me rot! I've borne great cost   15

Within this war, and as the leader of

My kingdom will appear there like a man.

I will not stay behind.

Enter Antony and Canidius

ENOBARBUS

Fine, I am done.

Here comes the Emperor.   20

ANTONY

I cannot fathom it, Canidius,

That Caesar could cross the Ionian Sea so quick

And occupy Toryne? You've heard this, sweet?

CLEOPATRA

Velocity is never more admired

Than by the dalliers.   25

ANTONY

A good rebuke,

For all to take to heart. Even the best
Of men grow slack. Canidius, we
Will fight with him by sea.

CLEOPATRA

By sea! What more? 30

CANIDIUS

Why by sea, my lord?

ANTONY

Because he dares us to it.

ENOBARBUS

Your ships are not well manned,
You've mule drivers for mariners, farm hands
From swift enlistment. But in Caesar's fleet 35
Are those that fought in many wars with Pompey;
Their ships are quick, yours heavy. No disgrace
Will touch you for refusing him at sea,
Being best fit for land.

ANTONY

By sea, by sea! 40

ENOBARBUS

Most worthy sir, you therein throw away
The unmatched soldiership you have by land;
You'll break apart your army, which consists
Of war-marked footmen; leave unexecuted
Your very own renowned prowess, and thus 45
Forgo the way of certain victory.

ANTONY

I'll fight at sea.

CLEOPATRA

I have sixty sails, unmatched by Caesar.

ANTONY

We'll burn our surplus ships, and with the rest,

Full-manned, engage approaching Caesar from   50
The head of Actium. But if we fail
At this, then we will fight on land.

Enter a Soldier

Yes, good soldier?

SOLDIER

Oh noble Emperor, do not fight by sea.
Do not trust shaky planks. Will you mistrust   55
My sword and battle scars? Let the Egyptians
And the Phoenicians go a-splashing; we
Have trained to conquer standing on the earth
And fighting foot to foot.

ANTONY

Sure, sure, away!   60

Exit Antony, Cleopatra, and Enobarbus

SOLDIER

By Hercules, I think that I am right.

CANIDIUS

Soldier, you are. But his plans do not grow
From where his true strength lies. Our leader's led,
And we are women's men.

Exit

ACT 3 ◆ SCENE 7

Enter Caesar and Taurus with his army, marching

CAESAR

Taurus!

TAURUS

My lord?

CAESAR

Do not attack by land; stay whole; Do not
Provoke another fight till we have won

75

At sea. Do not exceed this scroll's directive.   5

(gives him a scroll)

Our fortune lies upon this plan.

Exit

ACT 3 ◆ SCENE 8

Canidius marches with his land army one way over the stage,
and Taurus, the lieutenant of Caesar, the other way.
After their going in, is heard the noise of a sea-fight.

Alarum

Enter Enobarbus

ENOBARBUS

Lost, lost, all lost! I can't look any longer!
The Antoniad, Egypt's flagship, with all
Their sixty vessels, turns around and flies.
My eyes are blinded by the sight.

Enter Scarus

SCARUS

Gods and goddesses!   5

. ENOBARBUS

What's this passion?

SCARUS

The greater segment of the world is lost
Through imbecility. We've kissed away
Kingdoms and provinces.

ENOBARBUS

How did the fight appear?   10

SCARUS

As though our side erupted plague spots
That promise death. That ribald horse of Egypt —
May leprosy take her! — in the midst of battle,
When both sides had equal advantage like

76

A pair of twins, or rather ours the elder —   15
Hoists sails and flies at no more danger than
A gnat upon a cow in June.

ENOBARBUS

That I beheld.
My eyes were sickened at the sight and could not
Endure a further view.   20

SCARUS

Then once she fled,
The noble ruin of her magic, Antony,
Claps on his sea-wing and, like a doting mallard,
Flies after her, leaving the fight in height.
I never saw an action of such shame.   25
Experience, manhood, honor, never did
Betray itself so badly.

ENOBARBUS

Oh, alas!

ꙮ   *Enter Canidius*

CANIDIUS

Our fortune on the sea is out of breath
And sinks most lamentably. Had our general   30
Been what he knew — himself — we would have won.
Oh, with his flight he gives example for
Our own desertion.

ENOBARBUS

So you think that too?
Why then, it is goodnight for us indeed.   35

CANIDIUS

Toward Peloponnesus they have fled.

SCARUS

It's easy to get there, and there I'll wait
What fate brings next.

CANIDIUS

    To Caesar I'll surrender

    My soldiers and my horses.   40

ENOBARBUS

    I will still follow

    The wounded chance of Antony, though my reason

    Sits in the wind against me.

        Exit at one door Canidius, at the other Scarus and Enobarbus

ACT 3 ◆ SCENE 9

Enter Antony with Attendants

ANTONY

    Hark! The earth bids me tread no more upon it;

    It is ashamed to bear me. Friends, please gather.

    I am so darkened in the world that I

    Have lost my way forever. I have a ship

    Laden with gold. Take that, divide it. Flee   5

    And make your peace with Caesar.

ALL

    Flee? Not we.

ANTONY

    I've fled myself and turned you into cowards,

    To have you run and show your backs. Friends, leave.

    I have resolved myself upon a course   10

    Which has no need of you. Be gone.

    My treasure's in the harbor. Take it.

    Don't look sad,

    Nor make sounds of resistance; take direction

    From my despair's demands. Please leave the man   15

    Who has now left himself. To the harbor, go!

    I will bestow on you that ship and treasure.

    Leave me only some scraps — please do so now;

No, do so; for indeed I have lost command;
Therefore, please go. I'll see you by and by.   20

Exit attendants

Antony sits down

Enter Cleopatra led by Charmian, Iras, and Eros.

EROS

No, gentle madam, to him! Comfort him.

IRAS

Do, most dear queen.

CHARMIAN

Do. What else is there?

CLEOPATRA

Let me sit down. Oh, Juno!

ANTONY

No, no, no, no, no!   25

EROS

Do you see her, sir?

ANTONY

Oh damn, damn, damn!

CHARMIAN

Madam!

IRAS

Madam! Oh, good Empress!

EROS

Sir, sir!   30

ANTONY

Yes, my lord. Caesar at Philippi kept
His sword sheathed like a dancer, while I struck
The lean and wrinkled Cassius. It was I
Who killed the mad Brutus, while Caesar left
His fighting to his men, and saw no action   35
In the brave squares of war. Yet now — no matter.

CLEOPATRA

Ah, stand by.

EROS

The Queen, my lord! The Queen!

IRAS

Go to him, madam; speak to him.

He's unmanned by utter shame. 40

CLEOPATRA

Well then, sustain me. Oh!

EROS

Most noble sir, arise. The Queen approaches.

Her head's declined, and death will surely seize her

Unless your comfort makes the rescue.

ANTONY

I have destroyed my reputation, 45

A most unnoble swerving.

EROS

Sir, the Queen!

ANTONY

Oh, where did you lead me to, Egypt? See

How I attempt to hide my shame from you

By living in the glory of past deeds 50

Now ruined in dishonor.

CLEOPATRA

Oh, my lord,

Forgive my fearful sails! I did not think

You would have followed.

ANTONY

Egypt, you knew too well 55

My heart was to your rudder tied by strings,

So you would tow me on. You knew your full

Supremacy over my soul, and that

Your call would pull me even from the gods'
Commanding.   60

CLEOPATRA

Oh, my pardon!

ANTONY

Now I must
Send base entreaties to young Caesar; dodge
And haggle with the tricks of low men; I
Who once played as I pleased with half the world,   65
Making and marring fortunes. You did know
How much you were my conqueror, and that
My sword, made weak by my affection, would
Obey you, blind to cause.

CLEOPATRA

Pardon, pardon!   70

ANTONY

Let fall no tear, I say. One tear is worth
All that is won and lost. Give me a kiss.

(they kiss)

This alone repays me.
We sent my schoolmaster. Has he returned?
Love, I am full of lead. Bring in some wine   75
And food! Cruel fortune knows we scorn her most
When she most offers blows.

Exit

ACT 3 ◆ SCENE 10

Enter Caesar, Agrippa, Dolabella, and Thidius with others

CAESAR

Let him who comes from Antony appear.
Do you know him?

DOLABELLA

It is his schoolmaster;

It is a sign that he is plucked, that here

He sends so poor a feather of his wing; 5

He had superfluous kings for messengers

Not many moons gone by.

Enter Ambassador from Antony

CAESAR

Approach, and speak.

AMBASSADOR

Such as I am, I come from Antony.

I was before inconsequential to him. 10

As trivial as a drop of dew compared

To his grand sea.

CAESAR

Fine then. Complete your task.

AMBASSADOR

He bows to you, Lord of his fortunes, and

Requests to live in Egypt. If not granted, 15

He lessens his request and does entreat

You let him breathe between the heavens and earth,

A private man in Athens. That for him.

Next, Cleopatra does confess your greatness,

Submits herself to you, and of you craves 20

The royal throne of Egypt for her heirs,

Now at the mercy of your grace.

CAESAR

For Antony,

I have no ears to his request. The Queen

I'll grant her audience and her desires, 25

If she will drive her disgraced friend from Egypt

Or take his life there. She does this, then I

82

Will hear her pleas. Send this to both of them.

AMBASSADOR

Fortune pursue you!

CAESAR

Lead him through the lines.   30

Exit Ambassador, attended

(to Thidias)

It's time to try your eloquence. Dispatch.

Win Cleopatra from Mark Antony;

Pledge, on my word, what she desires; add more

From your invention. Women still are weak

In their best fortunes; need will always turn   35

The never-perjured virgin. Try your cunning.

THIDIAS

Caesar, I shall.

Exit

ACT 3 ◆ SCENE 11

Enter Cleopatra, Enobarbus, Charmian, and Iras

CLEOPATRA

What shall we do, Enobarbus?

ENOBARBUS

Brood, then die.

CLEOPATRA

Is Antony or I at fault for this?

ENOBARBUS

Antony only, who would make his lust

Lord of his reason. And though you fled   5

From that great face of war, whose battle lines

Frighted each other, why did he follow?

The shame of what he did was no less great

Than was the loss, to chase your flying flags

And leave his navy gazing. 10

CLEOPATRA

Peace, I beg you.

Enter the Ambassador with Antony

ANTONY

Is that his answer?

AMBASSADOR

Yes, my lord.

ANTONY

The Queen will have his courtesy, so long
As she would yield me up. 15

AMBASSADOR

He says so.

ANTONY

Let her know it.
To the boy Caesar send this grizzled head,
And he will fill your wishes to the brim
With territories. 20

CLEOPATRA

That fine head, my lord?

ANTONY

To him again! Tell him he wears the bloom
Of youth upon him, from which the world expects
Great future things. But his coin, ships, and legions
Are now a coward's, whose men would prevail 25
Under the service of a child as soon
As under Caesar. I dare him therefore
To lay his vain pretentions down and meet
Me as a man, sword against sword, ourselves
Alone. I'll write the challenge. Follow me. 30

Exit Antony and Ambassador

ENOBARBUS *(aside)*

    Oh yes, most likely that commanding Caesar

    Would risk his cheer, to be staged to the world

    Against a warrior! I can see men's judgments

    Are packaged with their fortunes: Ruinous

    Events will birth a ruin in their senses,   35

    To suffer out and in. That he should dream,

    Knowing men's measures, that full Caesar would

    Answer his empty station! Caesar, you have

    Subdued his judgment too.

Enter a Servant

SERVANT

    A messenger from Caesar.   40

CLEOPATRA

    What, no more ceremony anymore?

    See how a nose which smells a budding rose

    Stops short against a withered one. Admit him.

Exit Servant

ENOBARBUS *(aside)*

    My honesty and I begin to quarrel.

    Our loyalty to fools makes loyalty   45

    Mere folly. And yet he who can endure,

    To follow with allegiance a fallen lord,

    Will conquer that ill fate which grips his master,

    And earn his place in the books.

Enter Thidias

CLEOPATRA

    Caesar's will?   50

THIDIAS

    Hear it apart.

CLEOPATRA

    Say boldly. None but friends here.

THIDIAS

Perhaps they are friendly to Antony.

ENOBARBUS

He needs as many friends as Caesar has,

Or even we won't matter. If it pleases   55

Caesar, he'd leap to call him friend. And we,

Whose he we are, would be his friends as well.

THIDIAS

Thus to you, most renowned: Caesar entreats

You calm the worries in your head; he has

Control — there's no more thought past this.   60

CLEOPATRA

Oh, royal words!

THIDIAS

He knows that you embraced Antony not

From love, but rather that you feared him.

CLEOPATRA

Oh!

THIDIAS

The scars upon your honor, therefore, he   65

Does pity as compulsory blemishes,

Not as deserved.

CLEOPATRA

He is a god and knows

What is most true. My honor was not yielded

But conquered utterly.   70

ENOBARBUS *(aside)*

To be sure of that, I will ask Antony.

Sir, sir, you are so leaky

That we must leave you to your sinking, for

Your dearest quit you.

Exit Enobarbus

86

THIDIAS

    Do you have requests   75

    I can relay to Caesar? For he begs

    To be desired to give. It would so please him

    To let his fortunes make for you a staff

    To lean upon. It would most warm his spirits

    To hear from me you had left Antony   80

    And put yourself under his shroud,

    The universal landlord.

CLEOPATRA

    What's your name?

THIDIAS

    My name is Thidias.

CLEOPATRA

    Most kind messenger,   85

    Say as my representative to Caesar:

    I kiss his conquering hand. Tell him I'm ready

    To lay my crown down at his feet, and kneel

    Till from his all-commanding breath I hear

    The sentence of the Queen.   90

THIDIAS

    It's your best course. Give me grace to lay

    Homage upon your hand.

CLEOPATRA *(offers him her hand.)*

    Your Caesar's father Julius often

    Bestowed his lips on this unworthy place,

    As if it did rain kisses.   95

             Enter Antony and Enobarbus

ANTONY

    Favors? By Jove that thunders!

    What are you, fellow?

THIDIAS

One who but performs
The bidding of the fullest man and worthiest
To have command obeyed. 100

ENOBARBUS *(aside)*

You will be whipped.

ANTONY *(calls for servants.)*

Approach there! — Ah, you hawk! — Now, gods and devils,
Authority melts from me. Not long ago
When I cried "Ho!", kings would start forth
And cry "Your will?" 105

Enter Servant(s)

Have you no ears? I am
Antony still. Drag off this knave and whip him!

ENOBARBUS *(aside)*

It's safer playing with a lion's whelp
Than with an old one dying.

ANTONY

Moon and stars! 110
Whip him! If he were twenty of the greatest powers
Paying tribute to Caesar, if I found them
So saucy with the hand of she here — what's her name
Since she was Cleopatra? Whip him, fellows,
Till like a boy you see him cringe his face, 115
And whine aloud for mercy. Take him off!

THIDIAS

Mark Antony —

ANTONY

Tug him away! Then being whipped,
Bring him again. This knave of Caesar's will
Bear us a message to him. 120

Exit (servants) with Thidias

You were half withered when I met you. Well?
Have I left my pillow unpressed in Rome,
Forsook the getting of a lawful race
By Octavia, that gem, to be deceived
By one who looks on parasites?   125

CLEOPATRA

My good lord —

ANTONY

You have been a swayer ever.
But when in our corruption we grow hard —
Oh misery on it! — the gods sew up our eyes,
Submerge our clearer judgments in our filth.   130
Make us adore our errors as we strut
Straight to our ruin.

CLEOPATRA

Has it come to this?

ANTONY

I found you as a morsel, cold upon
Dead Julius Caesar's plate — you were a scrap   135
Of Gnaeus Pompey's, not to speak of lusts,
Unregistered in vulgar fame, you have
Most lecherously collected. For I'm sure,
Though you can guess what temperance might be,
You don't know what it is.   140

CLEOPATRA

Where does this come from?

ANTONY

To let a servant who takes others' scraps
And says "God bless you!" be familiar with
My playfellow — your hand — this kingly seal
And pledger of grand hearts! Oh that I were   145
Among the bulls of Basan, to outroar

89

The feral herd!

Enter a Servant with Thidias

Is he whipped?

SERVANT

Soundly, my lord.

ANTONY

He cried? And begged for pardon?   150

SERVANT

He did ask favor.

ANTONY *(to Thidias)*

If your father still lives, let him repent

You were not made his daughter; go return to Caesar;

Tell him of your reception. Tell him

He makes me angry at him, for he seems   155

Proud and disdainful, harping on what I am

And not what I once was. He makes me angry,

And at this time when it's most easy to do it,

When my good planets, once my former guides,

Have emptied out their orbs, and shot their fires   160

Into the abyss of hell. Away with your welts! Go!

Exit Thidias (with Servant)

CLEOPATRA

Are you done yet?

ANTONY

Alas, my earthly moon is now eclipsed

And that alone portends the fall of Antony.

CLEOPATRA

I must wait for him to finish.   165

ANTONY

To flatter Caesar would you mingle eyes

With one that ties his laces?

CLEOPATRA

Do you not know me yet?

ANTONY

Are you cold-hearted toward me?

CLEOPATRA

If I am,   170

Then from my cold heart make a poisoned hail

That heaven rains back down, and the first stone

Drop in my throat: and as it melts, then so

Dissolve my life! Next goes Caesarion, my son,

Till by degrees all issue from my womb,   175

And every last Egyptian 'cross my land

By the dissolving of this pelleted storm

Lies graveless, till the flies and gnats of Nile

Have eaten them for prey!

ANTONY

I am satisfied.   180

Caesar encamps in Alexandria, where

I will resist his fate. Our force by land

Has nobly held; our severed navy too

Has grouped again, afloat, threatening most sea-like.

Where have you been, my heart? Do you hear me?   185

If from the field I should return once more

To kiss these lips, I will be full-blooded.

I and my sword will earn our legacy.

There's hope here yet.

CLEOPATRA

That's my brave lord!   190

ANTONY

In muscle, heart, and breath I'll be three times

What I once was. For when my hours were lax

And lucky, men traded their lives from me

For jokes. But now, I'll fight. I'll bare my teeth
And send to darkness all who stop me. Come,   195
Let's have one final festive night. Call for
All my sad captains. Fill our bowls once more.
Let's mock the midnight bell.

CLEOPATRA

It is my birthday.
I thought that I should hold it poor, but since my lord   200
Is Antony again, I will be Cleopatra.

ANTONY

We will do well yet.

CLEOPATRA *(to Charmian and Iras)*

Call all his noble captains to my lord!

ANTONY

Do so, I'll speak to them; and tonight I'll make
The wine peep through their scars. Come on, my queen,   205
There's Springtime yet! The next time that I fight
I'll make Death love me, for I will contend
Even with his pestilent scythe.

Exit all but Enobarbus

ENOBARBUS

Now he'll outstare the lightning. To be frenzied
Is to be frighted out of fear, and in that mood   210
The dove will peck the eagle; I see how
A diminution in our captain's brain
Restores his heart. When valor preys on reason,
It eats the sword it fights with. I will seek
Some way to leave him.   215

Exit

ACT 4 ◆ SCENE 1

Enter Caesar, Agrippa, Maecenas, with his army,
Caesar reading a letter

CAESAR

He calls me boy, and scolds me as if he
Could beat me out of Egypt. He's whipped Thidius,
My messenger, with rods; and now dares me
To personal combat. Let the old ruffian know
I've better ways to die; and that I laugh   5
At his challenge.

MAECENAS

Caesar must know when one
So great begins to rage like this, it means
He's almost fallen. So give him no space
To breathe and make use of his madness.   10

CAESAR

Let our chiefs
Know that tomorrow's fight will be the last
Of many battles. In our ranks there are
Enough of Antony's former men that he
Must be defenseless. See it done, then feast   15
The army well. We have the stores and they
Have earned a night of waste. Poor Antony!

Exit

93

ACT 4 ◆ SCENE 2

Enter Antony, Cleopatra, Enobarbus, Charmian, Iras,
Alexas with others

ANTONY

He'll not fight with me, Enobarbus?

ENOBARBUS

No.

ANTONY

Why should he not?

ENOBARBUS

He thinks, being twenty times more fortunate,

He is twenty men to one. Why risk his lot? 5

ANTONY

Tomorrow, soldier,

By sea and land I'll fight. Either I'll live,

Or bathe my dying honor in the blood

That will restore it once again. Will you fight well?

ENOBARBUS

I'll strike, and cry "Winner take all!" 10

ANTONY

Well said! Come on!

Call forth my household servants.

Exit Alexas

Let's tonight

Be bounteous at our meal.

Enter three or four Servitors

Give me your hands. 15

You have been rightly faithful; so have you,

You, and you, and you. You have served me well

And kings have been your equals.

CLEOPATRA *(aside to Enobarbus)*

Why is he

Acting so strange?   20

ENOBARBUS *(aside to Cleopatra)*

They are those odd symptoms that sorrow shoots

Out of the mind.

ANTONY

And you are honorable too.

I wish my one self, Antony, was made

Of all your numbers, so I could perform   25

For all of you the scale of service you

Have done for me.

ALL THE SERVANTS

The gods forbid!

ANTONY

Well, my good fellows, wait on me tonight;

Do not give me a cup half-full, and treat me   30

As when my empire was your fellow too

And under my command.

CLEOPATRA *(aside to Enobarbus)*

Why does he do this?

ENOBARBUS *(aside to Cleopatra)*

To make his followers weep.

ANTONY

Tend me tonight.   35

Perhaps you've reached the end of your service,

And won't see me again, or if so, as

A mutilated ghost. Perhaps tomorrow

You'll serve another master. I look on you

As one who says goodbye. My fairest friends,   40

I do not turn you out, but, like a master

Married to your good service, stay with you

Till death. Tend me tonight two hours — no more —

And the gods reward you for it!

ENOBARBUS

Sir why do   45

You give them this distress? For look, they weep,

And I, an ass, am onion-eyed.

ANTONY

Oh, no, no!

May I be cursed if I meant you distress!

May grace grow where those teardrops fall! My friends,   50

You take me in too sad a sense, I spoke

These words to give you comfort, and desired you

To burn this night with revels. Know, my friends,

I hope well of tomorrow, and will lead you

To where I do expect victorious life   55

Rather than honorable death. Let's drink now, come.

And drown these cloudy thoughts.

Exit

ACT 4 ♦ SCENE 3

Enter through one door, First Soldier and his Company,
through the other door, Second Soldier

1 SOLDIER

Brother, good night. Tomorrow is the battle.

It's a brave army and full of strength and will.

Music of oboes is under the stage

2 SOLDIER

Shh! What noise?

1 SOLDIER

Music in the air.

3 SOLDIER

Under the earth.   5

1 SOLDIER

Quiet, I say! What should this mean?

2 SOLDIER

It's Hercules, who's Antony's patron god,

Who now leaves him.

3 SOLDIER

Do you hear, masters? Do you hear?

ALL

It's strange.   10

Exit

ACT 4 ◆ SCENE 4

Enter Antony and Cleopatra, with Charmian and others

ANTONY

Eros! My armor, Eros!

CLEOPATRA

Sleep some more.

ANTONY

No, my sweet. Eros! Come, my armor, Eros!

Enter Eros with armor

Come, good fellow, put the iron on.

If fortune is not ours today, we will   5

Defy her anyway. Come!

CLEOPATRA

Here, I'll help too.

What's this for?

ANTONY

Ah, let it be! You are

The armorer of my heart. No, no! This piece!   10

CLEOPATRA

Stop it. I'll help. It goes like this.

ANTONY

Good, good!

We will thrive now. You see, my good fellow?

Go put on your defenses.

EROS

Shortly, sir. 15

CLEOPATRA

Did I buckle this well?

ANTONY

Splendid, splendid!

Enter an armed Soldier

Good morning to you! Welcome!

Shout. Trumpets flourish.

Enter Captains and Soldiers

CAPTAIN

Good morning, General!

ALL THE SOLDIERS

Good morning, General. 20

ANTONY

This morning, like the spirit of a youth

Who means to be of note, begins early.

(to Cleopatra)

Fare you well, queen. Whatever comes of me,

This is a soldier's kiss. *(kisses her)*

I'll leave you, going like a man of steel. 25

Those men who stay with me follow me close.

I'll bring you to the battle. So, adieu.

Exit all but Cleopatra and Charmian

CHARMIAN

Will you retire to your chamber?

CLEOPATRA

Lead me.

He goes forth gallantly. If only he 30

And Caesar could determine this great war

With single combat. Then, Antony — but now — .

Well, on we go.

Exit

ACT 4 ◆ SCENE 5

Trumpets sound. Enter Antony and Eros, a soldier meeting them

SOLDIER

The gods make this a lucky day to Antony!

ANTONY

I wish you and your scars had once prevailed

On me to fight on land!

SOLDIER

Had you done so,

The kings that have deserted, and the soldier   5

That has left you this morning would have still

Followed your heels.

ANTONY

Who's gone this morning?

SOLDIER

Who? One always near you. Call for Enobarbus,

He will not hear you, or from Caesar's camp   10

Say "I'm not yours."

ANTONY

What are you saying?

SOLDIER

Sir,

He is with Caesar.

EROS

Sir, he's left behind   15

His chest and treasures.

ANTONY

So he's gone.

SOLDIER

Most certain.

ANTONY

Go, Eros, send his treasure after him.   20

Withhold no ounce, I charge you. Write to him —

I'll sign — gentle adieus and greetings to him.

Say that I wish he won't again find cause

To change a master. Oh, my cursed luck has

Corrupted honest men! Go now. — Enobarbus!   25

Exit

ACT 4 ◆ SCENE 6

Flourish

Enter Agrippa, Caesar, with Enobarbus and Dolabella

CAESAR

Go forth, Agrippa, and begin the fight.

I want Mark Antony taken alive.

Make it so known.

AGRIPPA

Caesar, I will.

Exit

CAESAR

The time of universal peace is near.   5

Prove this a prosperous day, and then the world

Now rended, shall bear olive trees.

Enter a Messenger

MESSENGER

Antony

Has come into the field.

CAESAR

Go charge Agrippa   10

Plant Antony's deserters front of line,

So he may seem to spit his fury back
Upon himself.

Exit all but Enobarbus

ENOBARBUS

Alexas left him too. As thanks,
Caesar then hanged him. Canidius and the rest   15
Who fell away have sound employment but
No honor and no trust. I have done ill,
Of which I do accuse myself so sorely
That I will joy no more.

Enter a Soldier of Caesar's

SOLDIER

Enobarbus, Antony   20
Has sent all of your treasures after you
With generous added gift. The messenger
Came on my watch, and at your tent is now
Unloading all his mules.

ENOBARBUS

I give it to you.   25

SOLDIER

Do not mock, Enobarbus.
It is no joke. It's best you safely guide
The bringer from this place. I must attend
My post or I would help. Your emperor
Continues still a Jove.   30

Exit

ENOBARBUS

I am the only villain of the earth,
I feel this baseness in me. Antony,
You store of bounty, how would you have paid
My better service, when you now have paid
My wickedness with gold! This blows my heart.   35

If grieving thoughts don't kill me, then I'll die
By grievous act. But darkest thoughts might do.
I fight against you? No, I will go seek
Some ditch wherein to die; the foulest pit
Best fits my latter part of life.   40

Exit

ACT 4 ◆ SCENE 7

Alarum

Drums and Trumpets

Enter Agrippa and others

AGRIPPA

Retreat! We have advanced ourselves too far.
Caesar is overwhelmed, our enemy
Exceeds what we expected.

Exit

Alarums

Enter Antony, and Scarus wounded

SCARUS

Oh my brave Emperor, this is real fighting!
Had we done this at first, we'd have driven   5
Them home with bandaged heads.

ANTONY

You're bleeding fast.

SCARUS

I had a wound here that was like a T
But now it's made an H.

Sound retreats far off

Enter Eros

EROS

They're running, sir, and our advantage drives   10
Us to an honorable victory.

SCARUS

Let's thrash their backs

And snatch 'em up as if we hunted hares!

It's fun to maul a coward.

ANTONY

I'll reward you   15

Once for your sprightly humor, and tenfold

For your good valor. Come on you!

SCARUS

I'll limp after.

Exit

ACT 4 ♦ **SCENE 8**

Alarum

Enter Antony again in a march; Scarus with others

ANTONY

We've driven him back to his camp. Run one

Ahead to let the Queen know of our deeds.

Exit a soldier

Tomorrow,

Before the sun sees us, we'll spill the blood

Of those who have escaped. I thank you all,   5

For you are valiant-handed, and have fought

As though it was your own cause, not just mine.

You men were warriors, each and every one.

Enter the city; hug your wives, your friends;

Tell them your feats, while they, with joyful tears,   10

Wash from your wounds the blood that stuck, and mend

Your honored gashes.

Enter Cleopatra

(to Scarus)

Here, give me your hand.

To this enchantress I'll commend your acts,
Make her thanks bless you.   15

(to Cleopatra)

Oh, you light of the world,
Embrace my armored neck! Pierce through my dress,
Through tested metal to my breast, and there
Ride on my chariot heart.

They embrace

CLEOPATRA

Oh lord of lords!   20
Oh infinite courage! You come smiling from
The world's great snare uncaught?

ANTONY

My nightingale,
We've beat them to their beds. Well, girl! Though gray hairs
Do mingle with my younger brown, I've still   25
A brain that nourishes my sinews and
Can score goals as a youth. Behold this man,
And let your favoring hand commend his lips.

(she offers Scarus her hand)

Kiss it, my warrior. He has fought today
As if he were a god in hate of all   30
Mankind, driven to purge us all.

CLEOPATRA

I'll give you, friend,
An armor all of gold. It was a king's.

ANTONY

He would deserve it if it were bejeweled
Like Phoebus's chariot. Give me your hand.   35
Through Alexandria we'll make jolly march;
Bear our hacked shields like the men who own them.
Trumpeters,

With brazen din batter the city's ear;
Mingle your trumpets with our rattling drums   40
So earth and heaven strike their sounds together,
Applauding our approach.

Trumpets sound

Exit

ACT 4 ◆ SCENE 9

Enter a Sentry and his Company of Watch
Enobarbus follows

SENTRY

If we are not relieved within this hour,
We must return to the guard house. The night
Is bright, and they say we will brace for battle
By the second hour of the morn.

1 WATCH

This last day was a sour one for us.   5

ENOBARBUS

Bear witness to me, night —

2 WATCH

Who is this man?

1 WATCH

Stand close and listen to him.

They stand aside

ENOBARBUS

Be witness to me, oh you blessed moon,
When hateful memories of men's betrayals   10
Are set upon the books, see Enobarbus
Repent under your gaze.

SENTRY

Enobarbus?

2 WATCH

Shh! Listen further.

ENOBARBUS

Oh moon, sovereign mistress of true sorrow,   15

The poisonous damp of night disponge upon me,

That life, of late a rebel to my will,

May hang no longer on me. Throw my heart,

Which is now dried with grief, against the flint

And hardness of my fault, where it will break   20

To powder, and put stop to my foul thoughts.

Oh Antony, more noble than my treason

Is infamous, forgive me in your soul.

But let the world rank me in register

A master-leaver and a fugitive.   25

Oh Antony! Oh Antony!

He sinks down

1 WATCH

Let's speak to him.

2 WATCH

Awake sir! Awake! Speak to us!

1 WATCH

Sir, do you hear?

SENTRY

The hand of death has caught him.   30

(drums afar off)

Hark! The drums

Now softly wake the troops. Let's bear him to

The court of guard. He is of note. Our shift

Is fully over.

Exit with the body

ACT 4 ◆ **SCENE 10**

Enter Antony and Scarus with their army

ANTONY

Their preparation is today by sea;

By land we do not please them.

SCARUS

We'll fight both.

ANTONY

I'd have them fight in fire or in the air;

We'd fight there too! But here: our infantry   5

Upon the hills adjoining to the city

Will stay with us — the order for sea is given;

Our ships have left the harbor —

Here in the hills we'll have good view to guide

Their next direction.   10

Exit

SCARUS

Swallows have built

Their nests in Cleopatra's sails. The soothsayers

Say they can't read the signs; but they look grim,

And dare not speak their knowledge. Antony is

Both valiant and dejected, and in fits   15

His checkered fortunes give him hope and fear

Of what he has and has not yet.

Enter Antony

ANTONY

All's lost!

This foul Egyptian has betrayed me.

My fleet has yielded to the foe, and there   20

They cast their caps up, and carouse together

Like friends long lost. Triple-turned whore! It's you

Who sold me out to Caesar. Now my heart

Makes only wars on you. Bid all retreat!
For when I am revenged upon my queen, 25
I will be done. Bid them all fly! Be gone!

Exit Scarus

Oh sun, I will not see your rising more.
Fortune and Antony part here; right here
Do we shake hands. All come to this!
I am betrayed. 30
Oh this false soul of Egypt! This deadly charm
Whose eyes launched forth my wars and called them home,
Whose bosom was my crown, my chief purpose,
Has like a scamming gipsy playing cards
Beguiled me to the very heart of loss. 35
Come, Eros, Eros!

Enter Cleopatra

Ah, you spell! Be gone!

CLEOPATRA

Why is my lord enraged against his love?

ANTONY

Vanish or I'll kill you as you deserve,
And rob Caesar's parade. Oh, let him take you 40
And hoist you up to the shouting plebeians!
Follow his chariot like the greatest stain
Of all your sex; most freak-like be displayed
For all the poorest people, for the dolts,
And let long-suffering Octavia 45
Plow up your visage with her waiting nails!

Exit Cleopatra

It's well that you are gone,
If it is well to live. But better you
Fell victim to my fury, for one death
Might have prevented many more. Come, Eros! 50

I wear the poisoned shirt of Hercules.
Teach me your rage, my ancestor;
Let me throw my betrayer to the moon,
Then with those hands that grasped the heaviest club
Subdue my worthiest self. But first the witch   55
Will die. She's sold me to the Roman boy
And I fall to this plot. She dies. Come Eros!

Exit

ACT 4 ◆ SCENE 11

Enter Cleopatra, Charmian, Iras, Mardian

CLEOPATRA

Help me, my women! Oh, he's more mad
Than Ajax for his shield.

CHARMIAN

To the tomb!
There lock yourself and send him word you are dead.
The greatness leaving from a man is more   5
Violent a split than soul and body parting.

CLEOPATRA

To the monument!
Mardian, go tell him I have slain myself.
Say that the last I spoke was "Antony,"
Please word it piteously. Go, Mardian,   10
And tell me how he takes my death. To the monument!

Exit

ACT 4 ◆ SCENE 12

Enter Antony and Eros

ANTONY

Eros, can you still see me?

EROS

Yes, noble lord.

ANTONY

Sometime we see a cloud that's like a dragon,

A vapor sometime like a bear or lion,

A towered citadel, a jutting rock,   5

A rocky mountain, or a blue headland

With trees upon it that nod to the world

And mock our eyes with air. You've seen these tricks?

They are dark evening's magic shows.

EROS

Yes, sir.   10

ANTONY

As quick as thought, that cloud that's now a horse,

The air dismembers, makes it indistinct,

As water looks in water.

EROS

Yes, my lord.

ANTONY

My good lad Eros, now your captain is   15

Like such a cloud. Here I am Antony,

Yet cannot hold this visible shape, my boy.

The Queen — I thought I had her heart, for she

Had my heart which, when still my own, annexed

A million beating more. Now they are gone.   20

I made these wars for *her*, while she played cards

With Caesar, then false-played my glory straight

Into an enemy's triumph.

No, don't weep, gentle Eros. I still have

Myself to end myself.   25

Enter Mardian

Oh your vile lady!

She has robbed me of my sword!

MARDIAN

No, Antony,
My mistress loved you and she bound her fortunes
With yours entirely.   30

ANTONY

Out, saucy eunuch! Peace!
She has betrayed me and will die the death.

MARDIAN

Death of one person can be paid but once,
And that she has discharged. What you would do
Has just been done for you. The last she spoke   35
Was "Antony! Most noble Antony!"
Then at last breath a tearing groan broke forth
And half the word Antony left her lips,
Completed in her heart. She took her life,
With your full name so buried inside her.   40

ANTONY

Dead, then?

MARDIAN

Dead.

ANTONY

Unarm me, Eros. The long day's task is done
And we must sleep.

(to Mardian)

That you depart here safe   45
Is payment for your labor. Go.

                    Exit Mardian

Off! Pluck these off!

(Eros unarms him)

Oh, cleave, my sides!
Heart, for once be stronger than your vessel;

Crack your frail case! Hurry, Eros, hurry!   50
No more a soldier; battered armor go;
You have been nobly borne. Leave me awhile.

Exit Eros

I'll overtake you, Cleopatra, and
Weep for my pardon. I go, for now the length
Of life is torture. So stop, and all is done.   55
Eros! — I come, my queen. — Eros! — Wait for me.
Where souls recline on flowers we'll join hands
And with our sprightly air make the ghosts gaze.
Come, Eros! Eros!

Enter Eros

EROS

What wish, my lord?   60

ANTONY

Since Cleopatra died,
I have lived in such dishonor that the gods
Detest my baseness. You're sworn, Eros, that when
The time comes that I should face persecution
Of base disgrace and horror, that on my   65
Command you'd kill me. Do it. For that time
Has come. You don't strike me, it's Caesar you
Defeat. Put courage in your cheek.

EROS

The gods forbid!

ANTONY

Eros,   70
Would you see from a window in great Rome
Your master thus, with bound arms, bending down
His conquered neck, his face subdued with shame
While fortunate Caesar, drawn before him in
A wheeled seat, brands with baseness all of those   75

Who walk behind?

EROS

I would not see it, sir.

ANTONY

Come then! For with a wound I must be cured.

Draw now your faithful sword, which you have worn

Most useful for your country.   80

EROS

Sir, don't make me!

ANTONY

When I freed you did I not make you swear

To do this when I bade you? Do it at once,

Or all your prior services become

Mere accidents unpurposed. Draw, and come!   85

EROS

Turn from me then that noble face

Wherein the worship of the whole world lies.

ANTONY *(turns from him)*

I'm ready! Go!

EROS

My sword is drawn.

ANTONY

Then let it do at once   90

The thing for which you've drawn it.

EROS

My dear master,

My captain, and my emperor, let me say,

Before I strike this bloody stroke, farewell.

ANTONY

It is said, man, and farewell.   95

EROS

Farewell, great chief. Shall I strike now?

ANTONY

Now, Eros.

EROS

Why, there then!

(kills himself)

Thus I do escape the sorrow

Of Antony's death.   100

ANTONY

Thrice nobler than myself!

You teach me, valiant Eros, by the thing

You could not do what I now must. My queen

And Eros by their brave instruction gained

On me in nobleness, but I'll still be   105

A bridegroom in my death and run into it,

As to a lover's bed. Come then! Now, Eros,

Your master dies your student. To do thus

(falls on his sword)

I learned from you. What, not dead? Not dead?

The guard, come! Oh, finish me.   110

        Enter a Company of the Guard, one of them Dercetus

1 GUARD

What's the noise?

ANTONY

I have done bad work, friends. Oh make an end

Of what I have begun.

2 GUARD

The star is fallen.

ANTONY

Let he who loves me strike me dead.   115

1 GUARD

Not I!

2 GUARD

Nor I!

3 GUARD

Nor any one!

Exit all the Guard but Dercetus

DERCETUS

Your death and fortunes make your followers fly.

This sword once shown to Caesar, with this news,   120

Will gain his favor.

Takes up Antony's sword

Enter Diomedes

DIOMEDES

Where's Antony?

DERCETUS

There, Diomedes, there!

DIOMEDES

He lives? Will you not answer, man?

Exit Dercetus with the sword of Antony

ANTONY

Are you there, Diomedes? Draw your sword and give me   125

Sufficing strokes for death.

DIOMEDES

Most perfect lord,

My mistress Cleopatra sent me to you.

ANTONY

When did she send you?

DIOMEDES

Now, my lord.   130

ANTONY

Where is she?

DIOMEDES

Locked in her monument. She had a prophesying fear

Of what has come to pass. When she first saw —
Which never will be proved — you wrongly thought
That she conspired with Caesar, and that your rage   135
Would not be purged, she sent word she was dead.
But fearing, with this news, what you might do,
She sent me to reveal the truth. I've come,
I dread, too late.

ANTONY

Too late, good Diomedes.   140
Bear me, good friends, to where Cleopatra bides.
It's the last service I'll command from you.

Exit, bearing Antony and Eros.

ACT 4 ♦ SCENE 13

Enter Cleopatra and her Maids aloft, with Charmian and Iras

CLEOPATRA

Oh Charmian, I will never leave this place.

CHARMIAN

Be comforted, dear madam.

CLEOPATRA

No, I will not.
All strange and terrible events are welcome;
It's comforts I despise. My size of sorrow,   5
When measured by its cause, must be as great
As the sad act that birthed it.

Enter Diomedes below

Is he dead?

DIOMEDES

His death's upon him, but not dead.
Look out over the far side of your tomb;   10
His guard has brought him there.

Enter below Antony borne by the Guard

116

CLEOPATRA

Oh sun,

Burn out your lamp so darkness will enshroud

The varying shore of the world! Oh Antony,

Antony, Antony! Help, Charmian! Help, Iras, help!   15

Help, friends below! Let's draw him to this place.

ANTONY

Peace!

Caesar's valor has not vanquished Antony,

But Antony's has triumphed on itself.

CLEOPATRA

So it should be that none but Antony   20

Should conquer Antony, but woe that it is so.

ANTONY

I am dying, Queen, dying. Only

I beg for death to wait awhile until

I may upon your lips lay the poor last

Of many thousand kisses.   25

CLEOPATRA

I dare not venture down to you,

Lest I am caught. The victory parade

Of the full-fortuned Caesar will not be

Adorned with me. I will be safe if serpents,

Knife, drugs have sting, edge, or operation.   30

But come, come Antony —

Help me, my women — we must draw you up.

Assist, good friends!

ANTONY

Oh quick, or I am gone!

CLEOPATRA

Here's sport indeed! How heavy my lord weighs!   35

My strength is gone from bearing heavy sorrow,

Made of such weight. Had I great Juno's power,
I'd make the strong-winged Mercury fetch you
And set you by Jove's side; but wishers are
The greatest fools. A little further! Come! 40

They heave Antony aloft to Cleopatra

Welcome! Don't die until you've truly lived,
And come alive with kissing. Had my lips
That power, I would wear them out like this.

Kisses him

ANTONY

I am dying, Egypt, dying.
Give me some wine and let me speak a little — 45

CLEOPATRA

No, let me speak, and let me curse so loud
That the false hussy Fortune breaks her wheel,
Outraged by my insult —

ANTONY

One word, sweet queen:
Seek safety from Caesar and keep your honor. 50

CLEOPATRA

Sometimes they cannot go together

ANTONY

Hear me.
Trust no one near Caesar but Proculeius.

CLEOPATRA

I'll trust my plan of action and my hands;
But none near Caesar. 55

ANTONY

Do not lament this miserable change
Of fortune at my end, but please your thoughts
In feeding them remembrance of the time
Wherein I lived the greatest prince of the world,

The noblest; know I do not basely die,   60
Did not cowardly bow my head to Caesar.
But I myself, a Roman by a Roman
Valiantly vanquished. Now my spirit is going;
I can no more.

CLEOPATRA

Noblest of men, will you die?   65
Have you no care of me? Shall I abide
In this dull world, which in your absence is
No better than a sty? Oh see, my women,
The crown of the earth does melt. My lord!

Antony dies

Oh withered is the garland of the war,   70
The soldier's flagpole fallen; boys and girls
Are level now with men, all measures gone,
And there is nothing left remarkable
Beneath the cycling moon.

She faints

CHARMIAN

Keep calm, lady!   75

IRAS

She's dead too, our sovereign.

CHARMIAN

Lady!

IRAS

Madam!

CHARMIAN

Oh, madam, madam, madam!

IRAS

Royal Egypt, Empress!   80

Cleopatra stirs

CHARMIAN

Hush, hush Iras.

CLEOPATRA

I'm now only a woman, and commanded
By such low passions as the maid that milks
And does the poorest chores. It would be just
To throw my scepter at the unjust gods   85
To tell them that our world did equal theirs
Until they stole our jewel. All is naught;
Quiet grief is foolish, but unruly tears
Befit a dog that's mad. So is it sin
To rush into the secret house of death   90
And dare death speed to us? How are you, women?
What, what, good cheer! Why, what now, Charmian?
My noble girls! Ah, women, women! Look,
My light is out, it's spent. Good maids, take heart.
We'll bury him, and then we'll do what's brave,   95
What's noble, in the high Roman fashion
And make death proud to take us. Come, away.
This case of that huge spirit now is cold.
Ah, women, women! Come, we have no friend
But courage and the swiftest end.   100

Exit, bearing off Antony's body

ACT 5 ◆ SCENE 1

Enter Caesar with his council of war:

Agrippa, Dolabella, Maecenas, Proculeius, Gallus

CAESAR

Go to him, Dolabella, urge surrender.

Being so beaten, tell him his delays

Mock only he himself.

DOLABELLA

Caesar, I shall.

Exit

Enter Dercetus with the sword of Antony

CAESAR

What's this? And who are you that dares appear   5

With blade unsheathed before me?

DERCETUS

I am Dercetus.

I served Mark Antony who was best worthy,

Best to be served. While he stood up and spoke

He was my master, and I wore my life   10

To war upon his haters. If you will

Take me, I'll be to Caesar as I was

To him. If this does not please you, I will

Yield up my life to you.

CAESAR

What are you saying?   15

DERCETUS

I say, oh Caesar, Antony is dead.

CAESAR

The breaking of so great a thing should make

A greater sound. The gentle world should have
Shook lions into civil streets and citizens
Into their dens. The death of Antony is not   20
The doom of just one man; in that name lay
A whole half of the world.

DERCETUS

He's dead, Caesar,
Not by a public minister of justice,
Nor by a hired knife; but that same hand   25
Which wrote his honor in the acts it did,
Has, with the courage lent it by his heart,
Splitted the heart. This is his sword;
I robbed his wound of it. Behold it stained
With his most noble blood.   30

CAESAR (*points to the sword*)

Look you, sad friends.
The gods may chide me for my tears, but this
Is news to wet the eyes of kings. Oh Antony,
I have pursued you to this; but we cut
The cancers from our bodies. Either you   35
Would look on my declining day, or I
On yours. We could not dwell together in
The whole world. And yet still let me lament
With tears as potent as the heart's own blood
That you, my brother and my partner in   40
The top plane of pursuit, my mate in empire,
Friend and companion in the front of war,
The arm of my own body, and the heart
From where my own drew fire, that our orbits,
Unreconciliable, should divide   45
Our equalness like this. Hear me, good friends —

Enter an Egyptian

122

But I'll continue at some better season.
The urgent business of this man is on
His face; I'll hear him out. Where are you from?

EGYPTIAN

A poor Egyptian still. The Queen, my mistress,   50
Confined in all that she has left, her tomb,
Desires instruction, and to know what you
Intend for her, so she may brace herself
To the way she's forced to.

CAESAR

Bid her have good heart.   55
She will soon know of me, from my good people,
How honorable and how kindly I
Intend for her. For Caesar can't incline
To be ungentle.

EGYPTIAN

So the gods protect you!   60

Exit

CAESAR

Come here, Proculeius. Go to and say
I purpose her no shame. Give her whatever
Assurances her mental state requires,
Lest, in her pride, with some mad mortal stroke,
She kills our plan. For she in Rome would be   65
The greatest trophy of our triumph.

PROCULEIUS

Caesar, I will.

Exit Proculeius

CAESAR

Come to my tent, where I will show you how
Unwillingly I was drawn into war,
How calm and gentle I proceeded in   70

My correspondence with dear Antony.
Come with me and you'll see.

Exit

ACT 5 ◆ SCENE 2

Enter Cleopatra, Charmian, and Iras

CLEOPATRA

My desolation starts to make me see
A better life. It's sorry to be Caesar.
Not being Fortune, he's but Fortune's slave,
A servant of her will.

Enter Proculeius

PROCULEIUS

Caesar sends greeting to the Queen of Egypt,   5
And bids you think upon what fair requests
You wish to have him grant you.

CLEOPATRA

What's your name?

PROCULEIUS

My name is Proculeius.

CLEOPATRA

Antony   10
Told me your name, said I should trust you, but
I do not greatly care if I'm deceived
Since I have no more use for trust. If Caesar
Would make a queen his beggar, tell him I,
To keep my majesty, must ask for no   15
Less than a kingdom. If it pleases him
To give me conquered Egypt for my son,
He'd give me so much of myself that I
Would kneel to him with thanks.

PROCULEIUS

    Be of good cheer. 20

    You've landed in a princely hand; fear nothing.

    Tell all your pleas most freely to my lord,

    Who is so full of mercy that it flows

    Over on all that need. I'll tell him of

    Your sweet dependency. 25

CLEOPATRA

    Tell him

    I am his fortune's slave, and recognize

    The greatness of his gains. I'm learning fast

    A doctrine of obedience, and would

    Most gladly meet him face to face. 30

PROCULEIUS

    I'll tell him.

    Have comfort, for I know your plight is pitied

    By him that caused it.

Enter Roman Soldiers

PROCULEIUS *(to the Soldiers)*

    You see how easily she may be ambushed.

    Guard her till Caesar comes. 35

IRAS

    Royal queen!

CHARMIAN

    Oh Cleopatra, you are taken, queen!

CLEOPATRA

    Quick, quick, good hands!

Draws a dagger

PROCULEIUS

    Hold, worthy lady, hold!

(disarms her)

    Do not do to yourself such wrong, for you 40

Are rescued, not entrapped.

CLEOPATRA

Where are you, Death? Come here, come, come!
One queen's worth more than your familiar piles
Of babes and beggars!

PROCULEIUS

Temperance, my lady!   45

CLEOPATRA

Sir, I will eat no food; I'll not drink, sir;
Nor will I sleep, even if I must babble
To stay awake. This mortal house I'll ruin,
Let Caesar do what he can. Know, sir, I
Will not wait pinioned at your master's court,   50
Nor even once be judged by the grave eye
Of dull Octavia. Shall they hoist me up
And put me on display to the shouting rabble
Of censuring Rome? I'd rather have a ditch
In Egypt be my grave! I'd rather lay   55
Stark naked on the mud banks of the Nile,
And host the eggs of water-flies who'd turn
My body ghastly. I would rather make
My country's highest pyramids my gallows
And hang me up in chains!   60

PROCULEIUS

You push these thoughts
Of horror much too far. Caesar's intentions
Should not give you this cause.

Enter Dolabella

DOLABELLA

Proculeius,
Caesar's informed of how you've done your job,   65
And he has sent for you. As for the Queen,

I'll place her with my guard.

PROCULEIUS

To serve Caesar

Has made my heart content. Be gentle to her.

(to Cleopatra)

I'll speak to Caesar what you please, if you   70

Will task me so.

CLEOPATRA

Tell him I wish to die.

Exit Proculeius with Soldiers

DOLABELLA

Most noble Empress, have you heard of me?

CLEOPATRA

I can't recall.

DOLABELLA

Assuredly you know me.   75

CLEOPATRA

No matter, sir, what I have heard or known.

You laugh when boys or women tell their dreams;

That is your habit, no?

DOLABELLA

I do not follow.

CLEOPATRA

I dreamt there was an Emperor Antony.   80

Oh, that I might have such another sleep,

To see this man again!

DOLABELLA

If it might please you —

CLEOPATRA

His face was heavenly, for his eyes were

A sun and moon which kept their course and lighted   85

The little earthly people.

DOLABELLA

Majesty —

CLEOPATRA

His legs straddled the ocean; his reared arm

Crested the world; his voice was harmonied

As all the well-tuned spheres, but when he meant   90

To shake the earth he was as rattling thunder.

His kindness was a harvest with no winter:

A strange and endless autumn which produced

More bounty by its reaping. His delights

Were dolphin-like: They leapt and bared themselves   95

Above the sea of war he swam in. Kings

And princes served him; realms and islands were

As change dropped from his pocket.

DOLABELLA

Cleopatra —

CLEOPATRA

Was there ever, or might there still be such   100

A man like this I've dreamt of?

DOLABELLA

Madam, no.

CLEOPATRA

You lie! Yet if there is or was this man,

He'd be past our capacity of dreaming.

DOLABELLA

Good madam,   105

Your loss is as great as yourself, you bear it

With royal gravity. If I don't feel

A rebound grief from yours that smites the root

Of my own heart, may I never achieve

Pursued success.   110

CLEOPATRA

    I thank you, sir.

    Do you know what Caesar intends with me?

DOLABELLA

    I'm loath to tell you what I wish you knew.

CLEOPATRA

    No, please sir.

DOLABELLA

    Though he's honorable —   115

CLEOPATRA

    He will

    Display me in his Victory Parade.

DOLABELLA

    Madam, he will. I know it.

Flourish

Enter Proculeius, Caesar, Gallus, Maecenas, and others of his train

ALL

    Make way, there! Caesar!

CAESAR

    Which is the Queen of Egypt?   120

DOLABELLA

    It is the Emperor, madam.

Cleopatra kneels

CAESAR

    Arise! You shall not kneel.

    I pray you rise. Rise, Egypt.

CLEOPATRA

    Sir, the gods

    Will have it so. My master and my lord   125

    I must obey.

She stands

CAESAR

    Have with you no hard thoughts.

    The record of what battle scars you gave me,

    Though written in my flesh, I shall remember

    As acts by fate's decree.   130

CLEOPATRA

    Sole master of

    The world, I can't argue my case so well

    As to absolve my blame, but do confess

    My acts betray those frailties which before

    Have often shamed our sex.   135

CAESAR

    Cleopatra, know

    I will excuse your faults rather than punish.

    If you commit yourself to my intents,

    Which towards you are most gentle, you shall find

    Great gain, but if you paint me with cruel colors   140

    By following in Antony's path of ruin

    You will lose all, and then deprive yourself

    Of my good treatment; you will put your children

    To that destruction which I'd guard them from

    If you're reliable. I will now take my leave.   145

CLEOPATRA

    And roam the world, for it is yours, and we,

    Your captured shields, your signs of conquest, shall

    Hang in whatever place you please.

CAESAR

    Don't make your thoughts your prisons. No, dear queen,

    For I intend to make of you my counsel   150

    To teach me how to serve you. Eat and rest.

    My care and pity are so much upon you

    That I remain your friend; and so, adieu.

CLEOPATRA

My master and my lord!

CAESAR

Not so. Adieu.   155

Flourish

Exit Caesar and his his train

CLEOPATRA

He words me, girls, he words me, so I should not

Be noble to myself. But listen, Charmian.

Whispers to Charmian

IRAS

The end, good lady. The bright day is done

And we are for the dark.

CLEOPATRA

Come quickly back.   160

I've made all the arrangements, it's prepared.

Go do it now with haste.

CHARMIAN

Madam, I will.

Enter Dolabella

DOLABELLA

Where is the Queen?

CHARMIAN

See, sir.   165

Exit

CLEOPATRA

Dolabella!

DOLABELLA

Madam: Caesar intends his journey

Through Syria, and within three days he

Will have you and your children seized and sent

To Rome. Make best use of this news.   170

CLEOPATRA

Dolabella,

I shall remain your debtor.

DOLABELLA

I, your servant.

Adieu, good queen.

Exit Dolabella

CLEOPATRA

Iras, what do you think? 175

You'll be displayed as an Egyptian minstrel

In Rome as well as I. Boorish workmen

With greasy aprons, sticks, and hammers will

Upraise us in the public. In their breaths,

Rank of gross diet, we will be enclouded 180

And forced to drink their odor.

IRAS

The gods forbid!

CLEOPATRA

No, that's certain.

IRAS

I'll never see it, for I'm sure my nails

Are stronger than my eyes! 185

CLEOPATRA

Yes, that's the way

To foil their preparation and to conquer

Their most absurd intents.

Enter Charmian

Now, Charmian!

Show me, my women, like a queen. Go fetch 190

My best attires. I'm going back to Cydnus,

The river where I first met Antony.

I'll meet him there again. Sweet Iras, go.

Now, noble Charmian, we'll swiftly execute,
And when you've done your chore, I'll give you leave   195
To play till doomsday. Bring my crown and all.

Exit Iras

(a noise within)

What is this noise?

Enter a Guardsman

GUARDSMAN

Here is a rural fellow
That will not be denied your highness's presence.
He brings you figs.   200

CLEOPATRA

Let him come in.

Exit Guardsman

How poor an instrument
To do a noble deed! He brings me liberty.
My resolution's fixed, no woman's frailty
Is left in me. I'm marble solid and   205
The shifting, fleeting mother moon is not
My planet anymore.

Enter Guardsman and Clown with a basket

GUARDSMAN

This is the man.

CLEOPATRA

Withdraw, and leave us.

Exit Guardsman

You have in there the Nile's pretty worm   210
That kills but does not pain?

CLOWN

Truly, I have him; but I would not be the party that should
desire you to touch him, for his bite is immemortal. Those bit
of it do seldom or never recover.

CLEOPATRA

Do you remember any who have died from it? 215

CLOWN

Very many; men, and women too. I heard of one of them just yesterday, no longer — a very honest woman, but somewhat given to lie, which a woman should not do if she is honest — I heard of how she died from being bit, what pain she felt. Truly, her tale makes good accounting of the worm; but he 220 who will believe all that is said, will never be saved by what he still may do. But this is most inevifallible: the worm's an odd worm.

CLEOPATRA

Get you gone. Farewell.

CLOWN

I wish you all joy of the worm. 225

Sets down his basket

CLEOPATRA

Farewell.

CLOWN

You must consider this, that the worm will do what he does.

CLEOPATRA

Yes, yes. Farewell.

CLOWN

Look, the worm is not to be trusted except in the keeping of wise people; for, indeed, there is no goodness in the worm. 230

CLEOPATRA

Please have no care; your warning's heeded.

CLOWN

Very good. Give it nothing, I pray you, for it is not worth the feeding.

CLEOPATRA

Will it eat me?

CLOWN

You must not think I am so simple; I know the devil himself 235
will not eat a woman. I know that a woman is a dish fit only
for the gods (if the devil did not dress the dish.) But even so,
these same whoreson devils do the gods great mischief with
their women, for with every ten women the gods make, the
devils ruin five. 240

CLEOPATRA

Well, get you gone. Farewell.

CLOWN

Yes, indeed. I wish you joy of the worm.

Exit

Enter Iras with a robe, crown, and other jewels

CLEOPATRA

Give me my robe. Put on my crown. I have
Immortal longings in me. Now I will
No longer drink the juice of Egypt's grape. 245

(the women dress her)

Quick, quick, good Iras! Quick! I think I hear
Antony call. I see him rouse himself
To praise my noble act. I hear him mock
The luck of Caesar; luck the gods grant men
For now, before their coming wrath. — Husband, I come! 250
My courage proves my title as your wife!
I am fire and air; my other elements
I give to baser life. — So, are you done?
Come then, and take the last warmth of my lips.
Farewell, kind Charmian. Iras, long farewell. 255

(Kisses them. Iras falls and dies)

Have I the asp in my lips? Did you fall?
If you and life can so easily part,
The touch of death is as a lover's pinch

Which hurts but is desired. Do you lie still?

CHARMIAN

Dissolve, thick cloud, and rain, so I may say   260

The gods themselves do weep!

CLEOPATRA

Her death deflates me.

If she first meets the dashing Antony,

He'll throw himself on her, and spend that kiss

Which is my heaven to have.   265

(to the asp; applying it to her breast)

Come, you deadly friend,

Untie this intrinsicate knot of life

At once with your sharp teeth. Poor venomed fool,

Be angry and dispatch. Oh! If you spoke

I'd hear you call our great Caesar an ass   270

Outfoxed!

CHARMIAN

Oh morning star!

CLEOPATRA

Quiet, quiet!

Do you not see my baby at my breast,

That sucks its nurse to sleep?   275

CHARMIAN

Oh break my heart!

CLEOPATRA

This poison is as sweet as balm, as soft

As air, as gentle — Oh Antony! I'll take you too.

(applies another asp to her arm)

Why should I stay —

Dies

CHARMIAN

In this vile world? So fare you well.   280

Now boast, Death, in your possession lies
A lass unparalleled. Soft windows, close,
The golden sun will never be beheld
Again by eyes so royal! Your crown's awry;
I'll fix it, and then I'll play in doomsday.   285

Enter the Guard, clattering in

1 GUARD

Where's the Queen?

CHARMIAN

Speak softly. Do not wake her.

1 GUARD

Caesar has sent —

CHARMIAN

Too slow a messenger.

(applies an asp)

Oh come quick! With haste. I feel you partly.   290

1 GUARD

What work is this, Charmian? Is it all done?

CHARMIAN

It is well done, and fitting for a princess
Descended of so many royal kings.
Ah, soldier!

Charmian dies

Enter Dolabella

ALL BUT CAESAR

Make a way for Caesar!   295

Enter Caesar and all his train, marching

DOLABELLA

Oh sir, you are indeed too sure a prophet:
What you feared is done.

CAESAR

Bravest 'til the end,

137

She gleaned my purposes and, being noble,
Took her own way. She looks like sleep,   300
Still apt to catch in her strong snare of beauty
Another Antony.

DOLABELLA

Here on her breast
There is a flow of blood, and some small swelling;
Another on her arm.   305

1 GUARD

This is an asp's trail, and these fig-leaves here
Have slime upon them such as the asp leaves
Upon the caves of Nile.

CAESAR

Most probable
That this is how she died, for her physician   310
Tells me she had pursued experiments
Of easy ways to die. Go to her bed,
And bear her body from the monument.
She shall be buried by her Antony.
No grave upon the earth shall hold in it   315
A pair so famous. Our army shall
In solemn show attend this funeral; then
To Rome. Come, Dolabella, see there is
High grandeur in this noble ceremony.

Exit all,
the Soldiers bearing the dead bodies